Premeditated Parenting

FOUNDATIONAL CHRISTIAN PARENTING
[TODDLERS-PRETEENS]

STEVE NELSON

A GREAT COMMISSION
NORTHWEST BOOK

Premeditated Parenting
FOUNDATIONAL CHRISTIAN PARENTING

Copyright 2006, by
Steve Nelson
801 37th Street
Evans, CO 80620
www.premeditatedparenting.net

All rights reserved. No part of this publication may be reproduced, transmitted in any form, by means of electronic, photocopying, or otherwise, without prior permission of the author.

All Scripture quotations, unless otherwise indicated are from the *Holy Bible, New International Version* © 1973, 1978, 1984 by International Bible Society. Used by permission of Zondervan Bible Publishers. All rights reserved.

Scripture quotations marked (KJV) are from the *Holy Bible King James Version*.

Scripture quotations marked (The Message) are from the *The Message*. © 1993, 1994, 1995, by Eugene H. Peterson. Used by permission of NavPress Publishing Group. All rights reserved.

Scriptures marked (NAS) are from the *New American Standard Bible*. © The Lockman Foundation 1960, 1962, 1963, 1968, 1971, 1972, 1973, 1975, 1977. All rights reserved.

Scripture quotations marked (NLT) are from the *Holy Bible, New Living Translation* © 1996. Used by permission of Tyndale House Publishers, Inc., Wheaton, IL 60189. All rights reserved.

Scripture quotations marked (NCV) are from the *New Century Version*. © 1987, 1988, 1991 by Word Publishing. All rights reserved.

Scripture quotations marked (TNIV) are from the *Holy Bible, Today's New International Version* © 2001 by International Bible Society. All rights reserved.

For the sake of clarification and consistency I have chosen to capitalize personal pronouns that refer to God, even when quoting from translations that do not follow this common practice.

ISBN# 0-9741008-1-1

Cover and layout design by Brad Dunbar
Back cover photo by Andrea Music

First Printing: May 2006

Printed by Kendall Printing Company
Greeley, Colorado 80631 USA

Thanks

A special thanks to my wife Kathleen. She has come up with, shaped, or tweaked everything contained in these pages. She is a special woman—far more so than I can describe here.

Thanks to John Meyer, Rick Whitney, Perry Paulding, Mark Darling and the other pastors in the Great Commission Association of Churches. What Kathleen and I have learned about parenting through all of you has shaped our family immensely. So many of the examples shared here have been given and used so much that I have no idea who came up with what. Although you won't get much acknowledgment, you do have our thanks. Many "ones" of us have been deeply impacted by your faith in action.

Thanks to our own parents for giving us a foundation of love and a reverence for God. We are grateful for a great start.

Thanks to CAR. You guys rock!

Foreword
– Rick Whitney

I am thrilled that Steve has written this book. We need more resources like it, written by involved dads.

For several years I have appreciated watching Steve and Kathleen's practical, common sense at work with their kids. I have appreciated their strong hearts and convictions. And I have especially appreciated their *"Never say we can't win!"* attitude.

Their children are still young, but the wisdom, and proven daily routines outlined in Steve's book really do work. The Nelsons are strong in their family schedules and habits, but there is also a whole lot of joy and laughter in their household.

When the foundations are strong, you can open up and experience even more grace and freedom as the years roll on. However, you need the foundations first.

Steve's directness and strength will challenge your thinking. He will stir you up. You might want to talk with him. He would be happy to. He really is a regular guy.

Steve Nelson, as a father and a pastor, desires that every Christian family wins with its own children. And probably the first thing we need to do to win is to believe that we can.

The Nelsons are looking for parents with strong hearts and strong will power.

I think you will be deeply encouraged by this book, especially if you are just getting started with your young family.

Keep pressing,

Rick Whitney
Regional Director
Great Commission Northwest

Foreword

– Laura Polk

I have had the privilege of knowing Steve and Kathleen Nelson for 13 years, and I lived with them for just over six of those. In that time I learned a tremendous amount and had the time of my life!

I've seen them apply the parenting principles written in this book with only one child, then two, and three, all the way up to number six. While each child has had a different temperament, with different strengths and weaknesses, I've seen that these principles work with each one.

The Nelson children are a joy to be around and a delight to spend time with. Moreover, they are secure, confident, happy children who deeply love each other, their parents, and God. They have character, a solid moral foundation, and get along well with others.

This is not the result of perfect parenting or a perfectly run household. In fact, what I love most about Steve and Kathleen is that they are a living testimony to the fact that you do not have to be perfect to have great kids. They are two of the most authentic, down-to-earth people I have ever known. If you ever visit their house you'll notice that the yard is dead and beyond much help. As you approach the door, if you happen to glance to the right you'll find an accumulation of Christmas trees from years past hidden behind the bushes. Dinners are not elaborate, usually consisting of a casserole, canned biscuits, and a frozen vegetable. De-cluttering means tossing as much as possible into the laundry room and shutting the door. On any given day you can walk into their home and find that a little one has usually forgotten to flush the toilet. This is encouraging to me, because I've realized you don't have to have it all together to produce great, godly kids.

I share all of this with great fondness, as I have learned from them what is important and where to be flexible. Their home is comfortable, a haven from this sometimes harsh world. It is filled with laughter, chaos, tears, joy, sorrow, "ow- ies", kisses, and lots of snuggles. Ultimately, you'll find it an "incubator of love," as one friend put it. I believe that the key to their success is attributed to daily living out God's Word in their home, giving their hearts to their kids and their roles as parents, and balance! There is a balance between love and discipline, work and play, and structure and flexibility, to name just a few.

I now have 2 (almost 3) children of my own and am trying to figure out, like you, how to win in parenting. Thankfully, my husband and I are not trying to figure this out alone. We've been extremely privileged to have Steve and Kathleen, and now their children (who have been an excellent example and influ- ence on children), as role models for our family.

Laura Polk
Friend of the Nelsons

Table of Contents

Introduction

Kathleen and I have six kids who, at the time of this writing, range in age from two to twelve. Just like the Brady Bunch, we have three boys and three girls, but unlike the Brady Bunch they are all ours. We are also excited to have another one on the way, which is really going to mess up the Brady Bunch thing. Kathleen is a home-mom, and I am a pastor at Summitview Community Church in Greeley, CO.

We've experienced countless precious moments with our kids—sweet prayers, steps of faith, and honest confessions. The older ones have shared their faith, are excited about God, and are developing their own deepening relationships with God. They are good kids. We are proud of all of them.

We've also caught one of our kids, about a year old at the time, sitting on the kitchen table with a box of cheerios dumped out around him. One of our girls cut her own hair once, which as you can imagine, did not go well. Several of them have written on the walls. Usually this occurs at an age when all they know how to write is their own name, so finding "persons of interest" in our investigations is usually not too difficult. We've caught them lying, stealing, cheating, yelling, hitting, threatening, biting, scheming, and doing most of the other "ings" kids do on occasion. Most of them have sampled a wide variety of deviancy over the years. These are not norms for our kids, but they are normal kids.

One time, I got so flustered at a kid, I became harsh and angry. Okay, so maybe it was more than once...

Let's get one thing straight. We are not perfect parents. If you were to watch our family for a week, you might think we were too strict. Some of you would think we were way too easy on our kids. We are also too affectionate, although I suppose a few would think we could be far more so. We've been accused of being too regimented even though we often parent in the midst of clutter, chaos, and shooting from the hip. Many will say that we take the Bible too literally, and some will be appalled at how we don't follow it closely enough. I have no doubt that we've broken most of the advice given in this book at one time or another. We have certainly made many mistakes and will continue to do so.

It's not about us, is it? It's about God. This book is about how God's principles have helped us as parents. We don't follow them perfectly, but we've been pleased with how God is shaping our children as we've tried to follow His principles in parenting.

This book is a mixture of our own advice and tips, as well as many timeless principles from God. The degree to which our advice lines up with God's Word is the degree to which this book will capture God's heart on parenting and have the greatest impact on your family.

Our hope is that this book will be a great springboard for you as you personally study out God's Word in these matters. You don't have to agree with Steve and Kathleen Nelson on everything. In fact, you'll undoubtedly *never* find a single set of parents that raise their children *exactly* as you think they should. That's okay. You don't have to agree with us on everything, but you do need to agree with God on everything. Before, during, and after reading this book, we strongly encourage you to develop a habit of studying the Bible. What you learn and apply from the Word will impact you more profoundly than anything you learn from any book on parenting.

> *Proverbs 3:5-6 Trust in the* LORD *with all your heart and lean not on your own understanding; in all your ways acknowledge Him, and He will make your paths straight.*

We hope that God will bless you as you read. This book is made up of lots of small articles. This made it easier for me to write during a free minute of time here and there. Hopefully that will make it easier for busy parents to read during a free minute of time here and there.

We warmly welcome you into our lives and our thoughts.

– 1 –

Rethinking Parenting

Sow a thought and you reap an act;
Sow an act and you reap a habit;
Sow a habit and you reap a character;
Sow a character and you reap a destiny.
— *Samuel Smiles*

A Heart for Parenting

"We haven't been able to revive her. You need to pray!" After about ten minutes of anxious waiting, that was the first medical report I had heard. I had felt a sense of dread for several hours already that night, and this announcement only made it more acute. Maybe that is common—I don't know—but I had an overwhelming feeling that I was going to lose either my wife or my baby girl.

I'm sure my fears would have seemed unfounded just minutes before. It had seemed like a routine delivery, but within minutes our whole lives came crashing down. The baby's heart rate suddenly dropped, and we were rushed into the operating room. I heard the doctor yelling, "Get the father away from the door," but I stood and watched anyway. The last words my wife heard were, "Knife up, stat!" and she drifted into unconsciousness. Kathleen was split open on the operating table before me, and our baby, Brea, was pulled out. Brea was taken just out of my sight into a corner of the room; however, I could still see some of the doctors and nurses attending her.

> *Nine months of hope, love, plans, prayers, and dreams died all at once.*

After several minutes, when I realized that they were still treating her, I actually thought, "Everything must be okay. She must still be alive." Only when I was asked to pray for my baby did I realize that they were working on her in a desperate panic and not as part of normal routine.

Another ten minutes passed before my fears were confirmed. Brea had passed away just before being delivered. I held her in my arms, but I knew she wasn't there. When Kathleen woke up, I had to tell her that Brea had died. It ripped my heart out. Nine months of hope, love, plans, prayers, and dreams died all at once. We cried all night long. In the morning I went home and told our other three children.

More tears. More pain.

Kathleen and I dealt with a flood of emotions over the next several months. It was hard to imagine how God could allow such a thing to happen. We had previously been devastated by the loss of three children due to miscarriage and, quite frankly, we thought God knew that we had been through enough.

Of course over time we realized that God had never promised to keep us from pain. We had an expectation on God that was unrealistic. We wanted this world to be what the next is supposed to be. In fact, heaven is described as being exactly what we were looking for—a place where God will wipe every tear from our eyes and where "there will be no more death, or mourning, or crying, or pain."[1] In our minds we had a picture of exactly how the world should be. However, what *should be*, and what *was* weren't lining up. Our hope was simply misplaced. We hoped this world would be like heaven, and it's not!

If we had truly lost forever a child we had never met, we would have been devastated beyond belief.

> *If we had truly lost forever a child we had never met, we would have been devastated beyond belief.*

---

[1] Revelation 21:4

Instead of being devastated, we were greatly comforted in knowing that our precious Brea was not gone forever but was simply in heaven. In fact, we were never robbed of her, but still have an eternity to spend with her. You see, our only *true* hope is in eternity. Paul wrote in the Bible, "If only for this life we have hope in Christ, we are to be pitied more than all men."[2] Hope in this life is futile. Because of our hope in eternal life, we have been able to go on, knowing that the things that are painfully absent from this life are the same things that make heaven all the more meaningful.

God's desire is that you, and that every single person, would spend eternity in heaven with Him.[3] Because that's what He wants, He's left us clear directions on how to get there. In fact, you can confidently *know* that you have eternal life.[4] The Bible says that you can never be *good enough* to get to heaven,[5] but that Christ died on the cross to pay for all the wrongs you've ever done.[6] That's the great thing about eternal life. It's dependent on what God did for you, not what you can do for Him. Jesus said that, "Everyone who believes in Him may have eternal life. For God so loved the world that He gave his one and only Son, that whoever believes in Him shall not perish but have eternal life."[7] By believing in Christ, and by trusting in what He did for you, you too can have eternal life and share in a hope that runs far deeper than any struggle you'll ever face.

That's the first parenting lesson. There's nothing more important than knowing where you and your family will spend eternity. If your children grow to be successful beyond your wildest dreams, but you don't get to spend eternity with them, you've missed the mark.

[2] 1 Corinthians 15:19
[3] 1 Timothy 2:3,4
[4] 1 John 5:13
[5] Ephesians 2:8,9; Titus 3:5
[6] 1 Peter 3:18; Romans 5:8
[7] John 3:16,17

I also share this story with you so you can see that I'm a real person. Like you, I have real hurts and real dreams. My kids are part of me. When they suffer, I suffer. When they take their first steps, I'm as proud as if I took them myself.

I remember when our first son was born. Our close friends came to visit minutes after delivery. I stepped out of the hospital room to greet them and was overcome with emotion. My eyes welled up, tears streamed down my face, and my voice cracked as I choked out the words, "It's a boy!" I loved my boy beyond description, and I still do. I love all my kids. Each one has a special place in my heart.

Like me, you have a heart for your kids. You love them like crazy and you want what is best for them. In each of them you see special characteristics, and you wonder just what kind of extraordinary lives God has planned for them. In some ways your kids might even be the embodiment of all your dreams.

Our kids can also be the embodiment of all our fears. We can almost feel that if they destroy their own lives they will simultaneously destroy our lives. A lot of dreams died the day that our little Brea died—a lot of dreams. Unfortunately, I've seen the parental dreams of many others shattered, not from death, but from rebelliousness. I've tried to comfort parents who have lost all control and most of their hope, and I've wondered if our loss was easier than theirs. The saddest thing is that their loss was avoidable.

That is why I'm passionate about parenting. Quite frankly, I'm brokenhearted from seeing well-meaning Christian parents grief-stricken by the choices of their children. God's Word offers so much hope for parents, not just to avoid heartache, but to experience the joy of seeing their kids follow hard after God.

Please permit me to speak strongly at times. I desperately care about you, your kids, and the reputation of God's character. I may fall into a fatherly tone at times. That's my thing and it's hard to tone it down when I feel so strongly about it!

I'd like to take the rest of the chapter to talk about the mindset of a successful parent. I've already shared some of my heart with you, and having a heart for your children is a critical element of being a good parent. It is also important to have a vision for the incredible calling that God has on your life. There are key aspects of parenting that we'll get to later like love, discipline, and training. However, how you mentally engage with parenting, its value, and its urgency, will greatly affect every element of your parenting.

The State of the Family

Imagine a 16-year-old boy who loves God and is considerate and respectful to you. He is faithful in his schoolwork, diligent at work, and involved at church. He is likeable, yet he cares more about what God thinks of him than about what his peers think. He has a deep and meaningful relationship with God, and his main goal in life is to live for Him and to spread His message. You could say he is a dream child. I believe that is a description of a man of God, and is the type of young man God would want us to raise.

I'm not concerned about *exactly* how that looks in each of my kids' lives. I understand that some will be more outgoing and some more reserved. They will all have varying degrees of success in the world. I imagine that some will even be more excited about God than others. Nevertheless, that is the basic picture in my mind of what I hope my kids grow into. That is what I will refer to as "winning" with my kids. Basically, God wants them to be like Jesus, and so do I. I don't expect them to be perfect by any means, but I do expect the influence of Christ to be undeniably obvious in their lives.

On the other hand, if my kids won't talk to me, don't have a vision for their lives, and have no interest in God, then I would say that I have lost that child—at least for a time. In the Bible, Eli, Samuel, David, and the father of the prodigal son are all examples of parents who lost their children.

In a future chapter we'll look at why we can have hope, even confidence, that we can win with our kids. But first let's evaluate the current state of parenting. I wish I could put a positive spin on it all, but I must be honest. I'm gravely concerned with the state of Christian families. I see that more are losing than winning, and I'm terrified that most parents aren't even aware of how dangerously far we've drifted from God's ideal. Consider the following letter:

Dear Friends in Christ,

I am not a member of your church, I belong to Peak Lutheran[8] in Estes Park, and I am appealing to churches in the state as a heartsick mother. I have two grown children. My daughter is an alcoholic and my son is a drug addict. I have done everything in my power to help them both. The only thing I can do is turn it over to God and pray. I feel that the more people that are praying for them the better. I feel like I am doing something constructive and it helps me feel better. My request is to ask for people to pray for them for three months. The prayer is this, "Dear God please surround Ben and Lisa with Your love, fill them with Your Holy Spirit. Keep them safe and sober."

Please do whatever you can with this request. God Bless your church, your staff and all who worship and praise in your holy house.

---

[8] Names and places have been changed.

I received this e-mail from a woman whom, as far as I know, I had never met and with whom I had no connection. Maybe she knew someone at our church, or perhaps she had found us on our website. I wondered if she, in complete desperation, was e-mailing every church in Colorado, faithfully collecting hundreds and eventually thousands of addresses, and crying over her keyboard as she faithfully worked on her rescue mission.

What was your initial response to her letter? I must confess that mine was judgmental. I had thoughts like, "It's a little bit late now," and "You should have thought about these things ten or twenty years ago." Don't get me wrong; I deeply admired her desire to do everything within her power to help her kids, but I thought she must have really missed it in the earlier years. (Obviously it is wrong to jump to judgmental conclusions. I'm not saying I was right. I'm just saying those thoughts jumped to my mind, likely because I've seen many parents who were uninvolved in their families until their family was in crisis mode.)

Perhaps she *had* been a poor parent. I don't know. Many parents aim for nothing and hit it. As sad as that is, that is not what troubles me the most about people's parenting. What really bothers me is that she may have been a relatively good parent. She may have taken her kids to Sunday school and church every week. She may have gone with them on mission trips and insisted that they were involved in youth group. She may have even been the best parent in her church. That is what scares me.

If we think we can simply parent at a respectable level and everything will turn out okay, then we need a wake-up call. I've seen too many "good" parents losing their kids to think that most Christians' current parenting methods are anywhere near the level at which they need to be. Someone recently asked me why some other speakers and I were using scare tactics, throwing around frightening statistics, and acting as if everyone was losing with their kids. The answer is pretty simple. It's because most people *are* losing with their kids, and we need a wake-up call.

I'm just calling it as I see it. I see too many teens who are apathetic toward God and disinterested in following His ways. I see too many cutters, drinkers, and drug users. There are too many depressed and suicidal teens and too many rebels. And these kids are coming out of seemingly healthy churches.

Maybe as a pastor I just hear too much about people's dirty laundry, but I've tried to be objective. Do you see something different? Are the majority of the teens in your church exemplary? Is your youth group turning the world upside-down? Are so many godly kids being raised up from within your church that your church has more leaders than it knows what to do with? Personally, I am not seeing marks of good parenting being left on our churches in great measure. In fact, I'm seeing the opposite. I'm not typically a reactionary person, but frankly, what I see frightens me, and there are statistics available that back those concerns.[9]

J believe that God has something radically better for us.

Please bear in mind that I am not writing to scare you. I'm writing because I believe that God has something radically better for us. However, to experience something different in parenting, it is imperative that we accurately assess the current state of the family. How we think about the state of parenting will profoundly impact both the sense of urgency and the

[9] George Barna, *Transforming Children into Spiritual Champions,* Ventura, CA: Regal, ©2003

intensity with which we parent. To experience better families we must parent better. For us to parent better requires that we see that there is a need to parent better. That is why it is critical that we see that the current state of the family is one of disarray.

> It is in unwavering adherence to God's ways that hope for the future of our families is found.

Embracing Extreme Parenting

You may just want a parenting tune-up or a few tips on how to make things a little better, but most families need far more than that. Permit me to exhort you: the parents that we see winning with their kids are of the no-holds-barred variety. In your own family you may want to consider an overhaul instead of a tune-up. Most families need to make immediate and significant changes. It is in unwavering adherence to God's ways that hope for the future of our families is found.

I thought about calling this book "Extreme Parenting," because to parent the way we suggest will certainly seem extreme to many. It takes extreme levels of determination, faith, commitment, and sacrifice. The reason I thought that title would send the wrong message is that "extreme" implies out of balance, or over the top. However, I don't believe we are doing anything beyond what God asks of us. While it may seem extreme by today's standards, it should be common practice among Christians—not "Extreme Parenting" but "Run of the

Mill Parenting." (And it goes without saying that no one wants a book called "Run of the Mill Parenting.")

Nevertheless, parenting as you should takes massive amounts of sacrifice. Many good mothers have given up their body shape, careers, sleep, and to some degree their sanity for the sake of their families. Likewise, many fathers have sacrificed promotions, wealth, and have even moved for the good of their children. (Okay, I admit it—most moms take the brunt of it. Thanks moms!)

Having kids comes at a cost, doesn't it? Isn't that why we think long and hard about whether or not we want more kids? We don't know if we want to be tied down for a few more years. We question if we want to work that hard, and we wonder if we can handle the challenge and the pressure. The fear of being the next family whose mother loses her mind or whose father ends it all because of financial pressures...well, we try not to even think about that.

Deuteronomy 7:14 He will love you and bless you and increase your numbers. He will bless the fruit of your womb, the crops of your land — your grain, new wine and oil — the calves of your herds and the lambs of your flocks in the land that He swore to your forefathers to give you.

It's interesting to note that God's blessings often come with increased pressure and work. In the above passage, God blesses by increasing the number of children, crops, and livestock. That's great, but that's more work, isn't it? It's more diapers, more runny noses, more weeds, more cultivating, more manure, and more animals breaking out of their pens. If you look at it from one angle it sounds great; if you look at it from another angle it can be depressing.

There is a church we occasionally drive by on Sunday

mornings that is as big as a high school. They even have traffic control officers managing the street in front of their building. Although I would love for our church to grow larger, when I drive by I silently pray, "Dear God, please don't ever let us get *that* big." I fear that degree of pressure and management, and I doubt my ability to endure it all.

Yet God sees increase as blessing.

Children are not an accident, a mistake, or a punishment. Biblically speaking, marriage is not just simply two people committing to each other. It is *God* joining two people together. In the same way, your children are not just byproducts of marriage; they are God's unique blessings to your family.

Whether you have one kid or ten kids, you need to line your thinking up with God's. The work that you do as a parent is work with which God has blessed you and which He has entrusted to you. It is important and meaningful work to Him. No matter what it seems like, or how hard it gets, God is pleased with your role as a parent. He sees it as a blessing—a good thing. If you're going to go the distance you'll need to come in line with how God sees your role and your work.

Being faithful with the blessings God has given you is not extreme parenting. That puts the focus on *your* work and sacrifice. It is extreme blessing. The focus needs to be on *His* provision. Your kids have been given to you by God, and He will provide the strength you need to manage the amount of blessing He gives you.

> *It's not extreme parenting but extreme blessing. The focus needs to be on God's provision, not your effort.*

If you can shift your thinking on this it will allow you to embrace your role as a parent. If you focus on all the work and sacrifice, your natural inclination will be to shrink back from your responsibilities. Parenting is God's crucially important mission that He has delegated to you because He wants to bless you and accomplish His purposes through your family. If you can view it as such you will be able to embrace parenting along with whatever challenges come with it.

Impact Parenting

Psalms 127:3-5 Children are a gift from the LORD; they are a reward from Him. Children born to a young man are like sharp arrows in a warrior's hands. How happy is the man whose quiver is full of them! He will not be put to shame when he confronts his accusers at the city gates. (NLT)

> *Parenting is God's crucially important mission that He has delegated to you because He wants to bless you and accomplish His purposes through your family.*

Of what significance are a warrior's arrows to him? They are his means of achieving victory. By shooting them with skill the enemy can be overcome, and the warrior's own life is extended. Solomon authored this particular Psalm, and in his day a victory for Israel would also be a victory for God. Unsuccessful warfare could bring shame to the name of God. There is a great deal riding on the successful deployment of one's arrows.

Our children are similar in several respects. Through them our life mission is continued. Our accomplishments and impact are multiplied through the children we successfully deploy. In a sense, our lives are extended through them, and they will continue to impact the world long after we are gone. If our children are successfully sent into the world, they will be great instruments for God. A genuine concern and love for people will mark their lives. They will share their faith with others and bring them to a saving faith in Christ. They will be church planters, community leaders, stellar employees, and model citizens. The lives of these children will bring glory to God. In essence, this is the magnificent part of parenting!

On the other hand, if our children are not successfully deployed into the world they may bring shame to God. They might demonstrate obvious outward signs of brokenness like drug use, drunkenness, truancy, or promiscuity, or they may struggle with more subtle issues like pride, greed, or complacency.

Many things affect the accuracy of an arrow. It could get intercepted in mid flight by another arrow. The wind could change its flight, or perhaps even changes in temperature or humidity could affect it slightly. However, the successful flight of the arrow primarily rests on two things—the quality of the arrow and the skill of the archer. As a parent, you have a great amount of influence on *both* of these areas—their character and your skill. The impact of your life and influence in this world will be significantly affected by your ability to mold and shape your kids and to successfully release them into the world.

Wouldn't it be heartening if the kids coming out of our churches were all life-changers? Imagine the impact if we were like an army of archers shooting our arrows into the world, spreading the gospel, showing love to the world, and doing acts of service. Just think of the potential impact. To be honest, sometimes I feel that instead of shooting our arrows skillfully like a trained army, we're more like blind men standing on a grease covered merry-go-round and shooting finless arrows. Something has got to change!

One thing that has got to change is that we must think strategically. We must understand that there is an impact from our parenting that is potentially world-changing. Our kids have limitless potential to be used by God in this world, and we would do well to think in these terms and equip our children accordingly.

A Call to Heroism

While a warrior must be brave at all times, there is a point at which a warrior must be reminded of the reasons for which he fights. He is already in the war, perhaps even in the battle, but then, in a moment of great need, the unthinkable is asked of him. It may be to charge a hill or capture a beach, but the outcome is almost certain. The mission will only be accomplished with great loss of life. His commanding officer reminds his men just what is at stake and just why each of them should risk their lives. And then with renewed bravery the warrior musters all his courage and puts it all on the line.

Nehemiah and Gideon each gave such calls of heroism to their men.

Nehemiah 4:14 After I looked things over, I stood up and said to the nobles, the officials and the rest of the people, "Don't be afraid of them. Remember the Lord, who is great and awesome, and fight for your brothers, your sons and your daughters, your wives and your homes."

Judges 7:18 "When I and all who are with me blow our trumpets, then from all around the camp blow yours and shout, 'For the LORD and for Gideon.'"

I am terrified by the complacency of parents that are taking a half-hearted, hands-off approach to parenting.

It's a similar call that I challenge you with now. Although you have already sacrificed as a parent, are you willing to take it to the next level? Are you willing to risk it all?

Nehemiah told his men to fight for their sons and daughters. In parenting, are we not also fighting for our children? I've received some very heartbreaking calls from parents—calls dealing with dropping grades, rebellion, police involvement, violence, and spiritual apathy. I hope our families are doing better than that, but men and women, I take this seriously. I am scared for our youth, and I am terrified by the complacency of parents who are taking a half-hearted, hands-off approach to parenting.

We need to think through what we are doing and what we need to do differently. We need to be serious-minded about this. We need to be wholehearted. There is much at stake!

Gideon told his men to fight for the LORD. Don't we also fight for the honor of our God? God's reputation is most certainly at stake within our families. If you've read this far, in all likelihood, you see yourself as part of a Christian family. What are your children going to tell the lost world about God? What are the fruits of your parenting going to tell the lost world about following God's principles? Do God's ways really work? Can they really be trusted? The lost world forms their answers to those questions by watching us, our children, and the results of our lives.

Like it or not, we are sending a message into the world. That may be more pressure than we care to shoulder, but, one way or the other, our lives communicate something about the realities of our beliefs. God wants us to send a message that brings His name honor.

The danger I'm addressing is that we may be like the soldier who has enlisted in the war, but is not mentally prepared for the battle. The state of our families and churches demands a level of heightened awareness of what we're up against.

It is amazing how parents rise to the challenge when their teen-ager is in full-fledged rebellion. They will do anything to save their child. Having the child change schools is considered. Moving or changing jobs becomes a viable option. Discipline is enforced at an intense level. Questionable friendships are discouraged. Clothing is monitored. Movies are censored. The parents will go to any extreme. Unfortunately, that is a difficult battle to win in the teen years, no matter how sincere the efforts.

> *Respond heroically now. Think in terms of a great task; everything is on the line, and there is no time to lose.*

Parent, are you willing to fight that battle *now* for the sake of your child and the honor of God? I know you would do it if the battle were more clearly upon you, but will you fight it now while your child is younger and so much more responsive? Year by year the battle closes upon you. Respond heroically now. Think in terms of a great task; everything is on the line, and there is no time to lose.

> There may not be a single event in your life that affects you more than having kids.

Premeditated Parenting

Parenting is a peculiar thing. Unlike many of life's other decisions, parenting is often entered into without a lot of forethought. When we think about what career we want, we give it much consideration. We reflect upon how a particular career will fit with our gifts and talents, we consider what kind of income we will need, and we weigh what type of school or training we will have to go through. When we get married, we often plan for months and go to marriage counseling and try to prepare ourselves for the difficult transition.

There may not be a single event in your life that affects you more than having kids. For most of us, it requires a total change in our level of self-sacrifice. It puts demands on our patience, sleep, marriage, and finances. When you become a mom or dad your child is completely and totally dependent on you. Perhaps for the first time in your life you become keenly aware of how your choices impact another individual. You can't just run off into the mountains and escape from the pressures of life anymore. That option comes at too high a cost. You're stuck here for at least eighteen years.

That's pretty serious! How is it that you need a license to

prune trees, cut hair, or unclog toilets, but anyone can be a parent? Shouldn't you have to take six weeks of pre-parenting classes like you do with marriage, or maybe a couple of community college courses? I'm not saying we should institutionalize parenting; I'm just saying that it seems like we don't give it much forethought.

For many of us, parenting was more of a byproduct of a relationship than it was something we consciously thought through. Perhaps we knew we wanted children, but we really had no idea of the demands it would have on our lives.

Perhaps what got us to this point is irrelevant. We are parents now! God has given us the charge of raising His little ones, and we need to carry out that charge faithfully. We need to take careful inventory of our lives. Where are we? Where do we want to be? How do we get there?

I call this premeditated parenting. I'm not talking about thinking through whether or not to have children. I'm talking about parenting. Pregnancy might be something that just happens to us, but parenting requires thoughtful and strategic planning. Having children is one thing, but raising them is quite another.

Pregnancy might be something that just happens to us, but parenting requires thoughtful and strategic planning.

I often worry that people raise children much like they do pets—just keep them fed and watered and don't let them irritate the neighbors too much. Keep their messes to a minimum, and train them enough to keep them somewhat enjoyable. A pat on the head here and there mixed in with a good scolding now and then should do the trick. That about sums it up for many parents.

That may create an 18-year-old, but that is unlikely to produce a man or woman of God, a spiritual champion, a good citizen, a leader, or even a good follower. Raising a child to physical maturity is fairly straightforward (if not nerve-wracking), but raising an 18-year-old world-changer is quite another matter. Many have given up on dreaming about raising a world-changer, but has God changed His plan? No, God still has great plans for each of our children.

Let's take this to a practical level. I'd like to ask you to do an exercise. Take out a piece of paper and start brainstorming some ideas of what characteristics you want your child to have when she turns 16. I know you're not worried about that yet, but don't you think it would be wise to develop that picture in your mind now so that you know what you are working toward? You could sit down and do it as an exercise with your spouse, or you could just stick a sheet of paper in this book or in your Bible, and jot down thoughts as they come to mind.

Throughout this chapter I've been trying to stress critical aspects of how we think about parenting. As parents, it is crucial that we have a mindset of seriousness and urgency. We must embrace our calling and grasp the significance of the task at hand. However, none of that really matters if it has not moved us enough to get up and get a pencil. (Remember, I warned you about that fatherly tone!)

You want to win and you desire great things for your child. All I'm asking is that you take a little effort now to start defining what that looks like to you. I mentioned earlier that some people aim at nothing and hit it. Let's aim for a bull's-eye. Let's think through an ideal picture of what we are aiming at. Then let's throw everything we've got at hitting it. If we end up being a little off target, then so be it. But we are sure to miss if we haven't even defined the target, and that is what I am asking you to do now.

With God's help we can rise to the challenge and take seriously the charge with which we've been entrusted.

1 Corinthians 4:2 Now it is required that those who have been given a trust must prove faithful.

Precarious Parenting Patterns

In our society there are mindsets and norms that people embrace that undermine successful parenting. If we desire a different outcome than our society, then we must be careful to not fall into the same thinking patterns that our society holds. Our culture holds a set of parenting values that is off base. However, these values are held by so many people that they seem normal. But normal is not what we're shooting for, is it? We don't want average kids; we want godly kids.

Here are a few well-intentioned goals that many parents seem to default to with their children. These goals are not all bad, but if over-emphasized they can detract greatly from the goal of developing followers of Christ.

1) A fun childhood.

Life is hard, isn't it? We face the pressures of life every day. We are under daily pressure to work and to pay the bills. The effects of sin tear apart our relationships and those around us. We read about horrors throughout the world. It seems like once you hit high school, if not sooner, you enter into a very different and harsh world.

Because of these realities, we are tempted to coddle our children and protect them from the ugliness of life. We may subconsciously think that every person deserves a happy childhood. As a result, we keep them from hard work and challenging situations. While we do need to protect the innocence of children and shield them from sin, we need to be careful not to pamper them by shielding them from all hardships in life.

> *Don't simply help your children have fun. Equip them for real life.*

A desire to coddle and protect can easily pull at the heart of parents, but it is backwards. Sure kids can have fun; I'm not against that. I want my kids to have a good life, but it is more important to equip children for the realities of life than it is to shelter them. Trying to make childhood blissful is like having Army basic training that focuses on the aspects of male bonding instead of equipping the soldiers for the battles they may face. Don't simply help your children have fun. Equip them for real life. They need to learn to work hard, to deal with difficult situations, and to persevere through hard times.

Even Jesus said that life would be difficult, and this is especially true of the life of a Christian.

John 16:33 "...In this world you will have trouble..."

In light of the reality of living in a trouble-filled world, childhood should be enjoyable, but not a fantasy land. Use their childhood to equip your kids for the real world by teaching them to do hard jobs and to stick it out in tough situations. If you don't, you'll miss the opportunity to train them for the difficulties of life.

I've got a little secret to let you in on. Kids are going to have fun whether you make it a priority or not. They are kids!

2) Self discovery.

When children are born, they are self-centered beings who want the world to revolve around them, and they pout and cry when it doesn't. If your goal is simply to help them discover who they are, they will become self-centered adults who fuss and cry when the world doesn't revolve around them. Your goal is to change who they are.

Genesis 8:21 [After the flood, the LORD *said,] "Never again will I curse the ground because of man, even though every inclination of his heart is evil from childhood."*

A child's natural state is not good. Your child's heart needs to be trained and shaped into something that is good. If we're talking about gifting or ability, then great! Help your child discover his gifts. However, if we're talking about heart and character, then by all means we must step in as parents and help that child not grow into a self-centered and vile adult.

If a child is left to himself, to turn into whatever he may become, do you know what happens? You end up with a child who is a shame to you and your God.

Proverbs 29:15b A child left to himself disgraces his mother.

> *Don't help them be who they are! Help them change who they are.*

You can foster natural abilities and gifts, but it is more important to shape your child's character. Don't help them *be* who they are! Help them *change* who they are.

3) Education.

I want my kids to be smart, to do well in school, and to test well—and so far they are doing great. I value education and we devote much of our effort as parents to education, but we don't see it as our chief goal in parenting.

Are the most well educated people in the world the best citizens? Are the churches flooded with the smartest people? Are prisons devoid of intelligent people? Undoubtedly, education brings enormous advantages into a person's life, but we would be dead wrong to think that it is some sort of cure-all.

> *Education helps with some things and is undoubtedly a good thing, but we're shooting for wisdom, not education.*

Have you ever had a rude doctor before? Smart people are definitely the ones you want when you're under the knife, but they're not always straight A people when it comes to life skills. Kathleen had a doctor once who had a hard time keeping staff because she lacked the basic life skill of being able to get along with others. Education is important, but it's not everything. Lots of people in prison can read. Education helps with some things and is undoubtedly a good thing, but we're shooting for wisdom, not education.

Proverbs 4:5-7 Get wisdom, get understanding; do not forget my words or swerve from them. Do not forsake wisdom, and she will protect you; love her, and she will watch over you. Wisdom is supreme; therefore get wisdom. Though it cost all you have, get understanding.

Wisdom involves the knowledge of right and wrong, not just true and false. Proverbs says that wisdom involves the fear of the LORD, humility, discernment, and understanding. Kids do need book smarts, but more importantly, they need life smarts.

4) Independence

Independence is a nice idea. If they end up being castaways, that will come in really handy. But for the other 99.99% of people, that's not useful, because we interact with people all the time! They will be naturally independent. Teach them how to be interdependent.

We typically want independence because we do not want to yield to the authority of others. We want to be the masters of our own lives. It's a spirit of rebelliousness, and it's the same spirit that makes your child or teen defy you. This doesn't need to be taught, it comes quite naturally.

Isaiah 53:6a We all, like sheep, have gone astray, each of us has turned to his own way.

This rebellion, or independent streak that we display, ruins everything in our lives. It ruins friendships, marriages, careers, and ultimately it cost Christ His life to pay for the sin that our independence brought into the world.

Ecclesiastes 4:9-10 Two are better than one, because

they have a good return for their work: If one falls
down, his friend can help him up. But pity the man
who falls and has no one to help him up!

We need other people in our lives, and they need us.
We do want our kids to be able to think for themselves and
provide for themselves. However, we also want our children to cheerfully yield to the authorities that God has put
into their lives, to humbly accept the input of others, and to
live lives of interdependence with other people.

5) Social acceptance

Like me, most parents have dreams of their kids excelling and being accepted by their peers.

We picked the name "Blaise" for our son chiefly because
of the quote from Blaise Pascal that says, "There is a God-
shaped vacuum in every heart." But "Blaise" (which we
pronounce as "Blaze") also has a certain ring to it doesn't
it? It's a good football name. I have a theory that much of
football revolves around names. You can win a Superbowl
with a quarterback named "Elway" or "Montana" because
those are football names. With a quarterback named
"Bubby Brister" your chances are greatly reduced. Now
if you change his name to "Bubba Brister" and make him
a linebacker, then your odds go way up. Anyway, you can
hear "Blaise" rolling off the tongue of the Monday Night
Football announcer, "And Blaise has the ball...he avoids one
tackler...and another... he has broken free and is 'blazing'
his way to a third touchdown."

What parent doesn't dream of their child excelling in
athletics, academics, or some other arena? But it goes beyond that. We want our kids to be cool, to fit in, and most
importantly, to not be made fun of. Again, I suppose those
are somewhat natural desires, but at what cost will those

desires be met?

If you want your child to fit in, it means they have to be like their peers. They have to dress like their friends, talk like their friends, and act like their friends. They can not be too smart or too dumb. It's okay if they are religious, but not too religious. They can hold standards, but must not hold on to them any longer than most kids.

I was not a particularly stellar teenager by any means, but one thing I was good at was working hard. I had a simple philosophy that if I was being paid to work, I should work. If I was on the clock and wasn't working, I was stealing by getting paid for doing nothing. And I also knew that I was simultaneously working for my employer and for God;[10] and God saw me even when my boss didn't. You would not believe the amount of grief I got for this in my early jobs. "Slow down, you're making us look bad," the choruses of the other employees would come. You wouldn't think working hard would be a particularly controversial stance, but it was. It made me stand out, and it made the other workers upset with me. It made it so that I did not fit in.

Now take this simple stance and add to it some other simple stances on drinking, premarital sex, modesty, honesty, and integrity, and what do you have? You have a kid that is not going to fit in.

It is true that we do not want our kids to be geeks. Who would? But it is more important to us that they be godly rather than fit in. Although I'm convinced that it doesn't have to be one or the other, I'd take a geeky but godly kid any day over a cool one that is immersed in this society.

As the Bible teaches, we do want to become "all things to all men" to present Christ's message in such a way that

---

[10] Colossians 3:23; Ephesians 6:7,8

we do not detract from it (1 Corinthians 9:22). However, it is also true that we are called to live as "aliens and strangers" in this world (1 Peter 2:11) and to "come out from them and be separate" (2 Corinthians 6:17).

How do we handle this balance? The obvious illustration of this balance is found in the life of Jesus. He was popular in that people were drawn to Him, His teachings, and His relationship to God. Yet Jesus never wavered on His standards.

Look at how the following passages show His connection with the people:

Luke 2:52 And Jesus grew in wisdom and stature, and in favor with God and men.

Mark 12:37b The large crowd listened to Him with delight.

Luke 13:17 When He said this, all His opponents were humiliated, but the people were delighted with all the wonderful things He was doing.

He was a friend of sinners and large crowds of people were drawn to Him. He also was willing to be separate from the crowds, and to stand alone for His Father.

Matthew 13:57a And they took offense at Him.

John 2:24-25 But Jesus would not entrust Himself to them, for He knew all men. He did not need man's testimony about man, for He knew what was in a man.

John 6:66 From this time many of His disciples turned back and no longer followed Him.

Jesus was willing to be separate. Jesus didn't have to be just like everyone else, and He didn't cater to their whims.

I do think it is good for our kids to fit into our culture to some extent. Their ability to reach out to the lost will be greatly hindered if they dress in robes and read from scrolls, but don't take this too far. John the Baptist strikes me as a little odd and he still had followers. Our kids don't have to carry iPods, cuss, or dress like hooligans to fit in. It is far more important that a Christ-likeness permeates their lives than that they fit in. Their character will be what draws other kids, not their coolness.

The main point to understand here is that our chief goal is to develop followers of Christ. They can have fun along the way, but fun is not the goal. They can discover their gifts, but self-discovery is not the goal. They need to be educated, but education is not the goal. I could go on, but you understand the point. The main thing needs to be the main thing, and that is developing followers of Christ. Keeping this emphasis clear in our minds guards us from the pitfalls of other well-intentioned goals.

FROM OUR HOME

Forward Thinking Parenting

Deuteronomy 4:9 Only be careful, and watch yourselves closely so that you do not forget the things your eyes have seen or let them slip from your heart as long as you live. Teach them to your children and to their children after them.

"When Mom dies I know what I want of hers," Silas proclaimed at the age of seven.

Since Kathleen's mom had died a year before, it wasn't a completely foreign topic to our house. Still, I was surprised and a little shocked that he would even contemplate such a matter. I prompted him to continue, and he said, "I want the picture of the little old lady she keeps in her Bible. I want to give it to *my* kids." I swelled up with pride that he would make such a sensible choice.

The picture he referred to is of a little old lady who was sitting outside of a community center after an earthquake in California. A tattered shawl is wrapped snugly around her head and falls down over her shoulders. It partially covers an old gray hooded sweatshirt which she is wearing over her dress. She is sitting sideways in a wooden folding chair, and in her wrinkled and age-spotted hands she holds open a Bible. In a time of tragedy she is experiencing the greatness of her God. There is nothing attractive about her, but she is undoubtedly a beautiful woman on the inside.

Kathleen put the picture in her Bible because she wants to have that kind of a heart for God when she is that age (which appears to be about 140).

I was touched by what Silas said, because he wasn't just interested in getting what was important to him, but he was interested in passing something on to his own children. He was already contemplating how to get his kids to grab onto the things that are grabbing his own young heart.

In a similar way, we need to be forward thinking in our parenting. We should be constantly plotting how we can pass on the special truths we've received to future generations.

– 2 –

Parenting with Confidence

Our beliefs about parenting are very important. They shape our passion, attitudes, motivation, and ability to persevere over the years. There is a temptation in parenting to look for the quick fix. If someone would just tell us what to do in each situation, we would be very satisfied. We all enjoy hearing practical ideas on parenting, but to parent successfully, we must wrestle through our beliefs in these matters. Continue to grapple with me through one more specific belief before we get into some of the practicals of parenting. One of the most important beliefs we must grasp as parents is that our parenting makes a difference.

Following Our Father

I suppose that in an ideal world we'd all come from perfect families, with perfect kids, perfect parents, and perfect pets. When it came time to be a parent you could just look back to your own childhood and follow the example of your own father and mother. And when you weren't sure what to do you could just call them up for advice. But we don't live in an ideal world, do we?

So who's your daddy now? Who are you going to look to for parenting advice?

The answer is that God is your daddy. He is your heavenly Father, and He created you. He also created your children, and has a great interest in your life and that of your family. God wants to help you. He wants to see your kids do well in life. In fact, did you know that one of the reasons your heavenly Father created marriage and made you one with your spouse was because "He was seeking godly offspring" (Malachi 2:15)? That doesn't mean that He wants all of your kids to be preachers. When He says He wants them to be godly, it means that He wants them to be true to Him, to have a heart and passion for Him, and to be men and women of character. He wants them to be more than just good kids; He wants them to be described as "godly"!

That's what you would like too, isn't it? You want godly kids, and God desires the same thing. He created you, He created your kids, and He knows what it takes to raise your children well. In James 1:5 it says, "But if any of you needs wisdom, you should ask God for it. He is generous and enjoys giving to all people, so He will give you wisdom." (NCV)

God has the wisdom you need; now you just need to get it from Him. Here are a couple of different ways to do that:

1) Pray for your kids.

The verse that we just read says that we need to ask God for wisdom. We ask by telling Him that we lack the wisdom we need to raise our kids well, and we ask Him to lead us. We can also ask by bringing specific situations to God in prayer, and then asking Him to give us wisdom in those situations. When little Johnnie leaves his books at school and they get stolen, should you buy him new books, make him buy his own books, or make him go without? The answer is easy...you should pray. Ask God to give you wisdom as to how to best use this event in Johnnie's life to teach him responsibility, without sacrificing his education in the process. Give it time. God will give you a great response.

Psalm 127:1 Unless the LORD builds the house, its builders labor in vain. Unless the LORD watches over the city, the watchmen stand guard in vain.

Remember, we are dependent upon God for success. Who is building your house? One way to measure whether you are trusting in God or in your own strength is to examine your prayer life. I know that may hurt, but we need to be honest with ourselves. Are we really seeking God for our families? We desperately need to pray for our kids!

2) Study the Bible.

The clearest way to know what God thinks is by looking at what God has already told you. Many of the passages related directly to parenting will be drawn out in this book, but it goes far beyond that. Not only does the Bible tell us how to parent, but how to live. It describes exactly what a Christian's life should look like, and that is the target we should be aiming for. We are raising our kids to be the godly men and women of character that the Bible describes.

God is your Father and advisor in parenting. He can lead you through prayer, the Word, and advice from other God-followers. Your confidence level in parenting rests on the foundation of your parenting. If your foundation is in God and in parenting His ways, then you can be confident that what you build upon that foundation will last.

> *Your confidence level in parenting rests on the foundation of your parenting.*

Getting Advice

You may have caught an interesting article in the news from September of 2004. During a hurricane in Florida, a group of people were in an office building riding out the storm. While they were trapped inside, a 54-year-old man ordered his pit bulls to attack these helpless people with the words, "Go get them!" One woman was bitten on the leg and a man suffered deep bites to his face and throat. After the initial attacks, they had to hide in their offices for an hour since the police were busy with hurricane-related activity. No motive was given for the attacks. The craziest part of the story was that this guy was a mental health counselor who treated anger management problems and addictions. His past arrests included aggravated assault with a weapon, domestic violence, and sexual assault. Now doesn't that sound like the kind of guy you'd like to visit for your anger issues? You'd sure want to be careful not to tick him off from the counseling couch!

Now I don't think all anger management counselors act in this way, anymore than I would think that type of behavior is typical of all 54-year-olds, or even all men. We can't stereotype all counselors as bad, and I certainly don't want to be included in many of the stereotypes of pastors! However, this story does illustrate this point well: you sure want to be careful who you go to for advice! Can you imagine the counseling sessions? "Well Steve, when I get angry here's how I like to let off a little steam..."

Proverbs 15:22 says, "Plans fail for lack of counsel, but with many advisers they succeed." We need advice, and that advice needs to be from people who are following God's principles in their own parenting. We must be careful here about who we are following. Our culture offers lots of advice, most of which is significantly divergent from God's recommendations. The advice we seek should not be from the world's experts but from those who are successfully following God.

Proverbs 12:5 The plans of the righteous are just, but the advice of the wicked is deceitful.

Who do you go to for parenting advice? Many people just pick up a book or a magazine and have no idea what type of parent the author is. The author may or may not be a good parent, or may not even be a parent at all! He or she may not use biblical principles or may even use Scripture selectively to support a personal agenda. Here are some things you should consider whenever you get parenting advice:

- Do you know him/her personally? (It's easy to look good at a distance!)
- Does he/she have kids you'd like your kids imitate?
- Does he/she have a life that you'd like to imitate?
- Is he/she winning with his/her own kids?

- Even better: Has he/she already won with his/her own kids?
- Does he/she go to the Bible for answers, or merely express personal opinions that sound Christian-based?

Where do the people who currently influence your life get the majority of their input? Should you be listening to them? Parenting can be grueling work! Parents can be hungry for answers, and it's tempting to lend an ear to anyone with an opinion, a word of hope, or a few initials behind their name. Some people listen to us just because we have a large number of kids. Trust me, having lots of kids does not demonstrate that you are a good parent; it just shows that you are fertile. As long as good advice is being given, then it is great to listen to others. But how do we know that good advice is being given? I'd like to have confidence in the input we receive.

The ideal situation is to get advice from couples in your church whom you know and respect and who have kids you admire. If you don't know those things about a family, then how do you know if their advice is really on target? Not only that, but if you know them and they know you, then the chances of getting good advice are greatly increased. Do you need to seek out other mentors in your life to get the input you need?

Of course, the same goes for my wife and me. Unless you know us, we are just two more voices among thousands. I'm certainly not trying to get you to put down this book! If you'll keep reading, I'll keep writing! However, I encourage you to have people actively involved in your life whom you know and who know you—people whose lives are heading where you want to go and who can mentor you in parenting, marriage, and in all aspects of the Christian life. Don't trust every expert! Don't even trust every Christian author. Instead, look around you. Who is going before you? Who do you know that is living out the Christian life in such a way that it has profoundly impacted their parenting? Seek their help, get their advice and feedback, and imitate their faith.

> *Who do you know that is living out the Christian life in such a way that it has profoundly impacted their parenting?*

1 Thessalonians 5:21 Test everything. Hold on to the good.

Hebrews 13:7 Remember your leaders, who spoke the word of God to you. Consider the outcome of their way of life and imitate their faith.

Why Do Bad Kids Happen to Good Parents?

A myth exists in Christian circles that when it really comes down to it, you can't truly have much impact on the outcome of your children. People think that you can raise them right and invest eighteen years of your life into them, but when they hit their upper teen years anything can (and will) happen.

This is a fundamental issue to address in parenting because, if it is true, then why in the world would any parent pour his or her heart, soul, energy, and life into parenting? Seeing the light at the end of the tunnel is a key motivator for most of us. Why would an athlete train if he didn't have hope of improving? Why would a student study if she had no hope of learning, graduating, or applying the material? We need to know that our efforts will pay off at some point. If there is no guarantee of how our kids will turn out, then there is little motivation to parent wholeheartedly.

So, what's the truth? Well, we need to start by realizing that any good lie has a great deal of truth mixed in with it. Blatant lies are much more easily spotted than ones laced with truth, and, like any good lie, this one has much truth to it. So, before addressing why we can have confidence in the outcome of our children, let's address why we can doubt that truth.

One of the reasons we doubt that we can have a profound impact on the outcome of our kids is that sometimes it seems as if bad kids are coming out of good families. I've seen many good parents who have had kids that didn't turn out well. I've also seen some kids with admirable character who came out of messed up families. From outward appearances it would be pretty easy to deduce that parents can't control the outcome of their kids very well.

So from outward appearances is it safe to deduce that we can't guarantee the outcome of our children? That is an important question to consider, but I'd also say that appearances are deceiving. Over the past few decades family values have eroded in both Christian and non-Christian homes. Perhaps what we think of as a good home is only good in comparison to other homes. It is possible that many "good homes" are not really all that great. It may be that the standards in the average Christian home are so far off that they're not worth looking to for what works and what doesn't.

That is my opinion. I think many Christian parents try hard and fail miserably. I'm not saying that every parent who goes through tough times, or who has had a child turn from God, has failed miserably. I don't believe that. But few parents really nail it with parenting. They put in time, energy, and effort, but they don't nail it. Is it proud to say that we can succeed where others have failed? It is if we are basing our confidence on our own efforts and programs. However, if the belief in the future success of our children is based on what God says, then that is not pride at all! It is faith.

I'm not good at losing weight. Most people I know are not good at losing weight. Some people I know eat very little and are still overweight. Others eat a lot and never gain any weight. However, it would be wrong to issue a blanket statement that we really have no control over our weight. We all know, when it comes right down to it, that the issue of weight loss is simply a matter of exercise and diet. Some people are exceptions to the rule, like those with health issues, but for most of us, exercise and diet is the key to weight loss. In the same way, in parenting you should not fear (or take comfort in) the failures of others. Just because many parents are failing does not mean that we should issue a blanket statement that says, "Parenting does not work. You cannot control how your kids turn out." On the contrary, just as in dieting, there are principles that will bring great success for the vast majority of the parents who apply them. Could there be exceptions? Sure. There may be exceptions to the rule, but the rule should be this: When Christian parents use biblical parenting principles year after year, it will produce godly kids who become godly adults. I'm every bit as

> When Christian parents use biblical parenting principles year after year, it will produce godly kids who become godly adults.

confident of that as the fact that if I diet and exercise, I *will* lose weight.

Does Free Will Contradict Confident Parenting?

Another common argument for the case that you can't dictate the outcome of your children's lives is the issue of free will. The concept of free will is simply this: God has created each of us with the ability to choose. I am not forced to make any choice based upon anyone else's will—not God's, not the government's, and not my parents'. The choice is mine. Of course, God, the government, and my parents may dictate consequences for certain actions to help me make wise choices, but that is another topic. The point is that your children have choices. They will have to choose to become Christians, resist peer pressure, refrain from premarital sex, and correctly make countless other choices. You cannot make those choices for your kids.

Some people put it this way, "Adam messed up, didn't he? And who was his parent? You don't think you can parent better than God, do you?" (By the way, it's a flawed analogy. Adam was neither raised by God, nor was he necessarily all that bad of a person by the standards we are talking about.)

The issue of free will is truly difficult. How can I have any confidence in how my kids turn out when I know that they have free will? This is a point worth consideration and it may explain why there seem to be exceptions to the rule that biblical parenting principles will produce godly kids.

Even though your kids will always have free will, you have an incredible amount of influence on their will. We expect teachers to impact students, officers to train soldiers, and coaches to influence athletes. Why wouldn't we expect parents to impact their kids? Students, soldiers, and athletes all have free will, and yet they are greatly influenced by those over them. Jesus said, "A student is not above his teacher, but everyone who is fully trained *will* be like his teacher." (Luke 6:40) Why wouldn't we expect the same thing from a parent who spends 18 years *training* his or her children?

One might ask, "What about Judas? Wasn't he trained by Jesus? Didn't his free will win out?" That's a good point to which I have three responses. First of all, if Christians today "lost" only one out of every twelve of their children I'd be much more encouraged with the situation than I am now. Secondly, it seems as if Judas may have been chosen as a disciple not to be a disciple, but for the very purpose of betraying Jesus and fulfilling Scripture (John 17:12). Thirdly, most of us would agree that Judas wasn't "fully trained" as referred to in the verse when it says, "Everyone who is fully trained *will* be like his teacher." Had Judas been Jesus' son (sounds like a great Star Wars plot) I most certainly would not have expected that kind of outcome from his life.

> *Yes, they have free will, but you can greatly influence that will.*

If you do a good job raising your kids, they will be much more likely to be model citizens than if you don't. Your kids should be far more likely to be following God than to become atheists. They should be far more likely to be doctors, missionaries, and judges than to turn out to be frauds, serial killers, or terrorists. Why? Your example, training, and influence are shaping them. Yes, they have free will. But you can greatly influence that will, just as your parents, teachers, and Sunday school teachers have greatly influenced you—for the better or for the worse.

FROM OUR HOME

Where We Lack God Supplies

Did I mention that I am not perfect? I think it is time that I build my case.

When Hope was little, just barely old enough to roll over, I set her down on our bed for a nap. (I can already feel the scorn of mothers everywhere. Dads, let me explain: a child that is old enough to roll should not be set on a bed. That is why we have cribs.)

As is usual for a child her age, she cried as I turned off the light and shut the door. Then she cried some more, and a little more after that, and then after a few minutes she settled into a full-blown wail. I knew better than to go and check on her. "Once you crack that door open she's never going to let you put her down," I thought to myself. I checked the clock and decided to let her try to cry herself to sleep for ten minutes.

After ten minutes passed she was still crying uncontrollably. I cautiously cracked the door open and peeked inside, but I could not locate her in the dark. I carefully edged the door open a little farther, but I still could not see her. Suddenly fearing that she had fallen off the bed, I flung the door open to rescue her. I made a quick scan of the bed and discovered that yes, indeed, she had fallen. Unfortunately, I did not see her on the floor. The only place left to look was under the bed, and sure enough... she was not there either.

I could still hear her crying, so I knew she couldn't be too far away. All I had to do was listen. After all, how many places can you hide in a 10' x 10' bedroom when rolling is the only mode of transportation you've mastered?

Although her cries were somewhat muffled, I eventually discovered her at the foot of the bed…in a laundry basket…headfirst. Guys, quit laughing. Women, I beg you, give me another chance. That was over ten years ago. Of course, Kathleen hasn't let me watch the kids since then either. Just kidding. She does leave me with the kids, but for some strange reason I get a detailed explanation of basic childcare every time she leaves. But trust me! I'm a much wiser parent now!

Although we can laugh about it now, I understand how foolish and serious my mistake was. If Hope had stopped crying I would not have checked on her until she had suffocated. Our treasured family tale could have just as easily been a painful story of shame.

We've all made mistakes, not just related to the safety of our children, but in every aspect of our parenting. We make mistakes in what we let our kids watch and do, who they associate with, and how we interact with them. All of our mistakes could potentially be costly. None of us will parent perfectly, but God, in His grace, can certainly make up where we lack.

I take great comfort in the following verse:

2 Corinthians 12:9 But He said to me, "My grace is sufficient for you, for my power is made perfect in weakness." Therefore I will boast all the more gladly about my weaknesses, so that Christ's power may rest on me.

What Guarantees Do You Have?

Let's look a little more into the question that we looked at earlier. Why in the world would any parent pour his or her heart, soul, energy, and life into parenting? Of course, the answer (or maybe one answer) is that we can greatly influence them, and that through them we can greatly influence the world. However, the question still remains. Can we be guaranteed of success?

The verse commonly used to encourage parents and to give them hope is the following:

Proverbs 22:6 Train a child in the way he should go, and when he is old he will not turn from it.

This verse quite clearly states that if you set children down a certain course, they will continue down that course. Yet most of us have seen families that appear to be exceptions to this verse, and, as a result, our faith in its reliability can be challenged.

If this verse does not at first seem to ring true to us, what do we do with it?

We can:

1) Redefine it.

Maybe we need to redefine some of the terms. Perhaps "He will not turn from it" doesn't mean that he will follow it, but just that he will not reject it. Or maybe "train" incorporates the idea that they have not just been taught, but have accepted and followed the teaching—in which case following the teaching and being trained go hand-in-hand. I'm sure there are other words or phrases we could redefine as well.

The problem with this approach is that, if you play with the words too much, the verse gets so watered down that it loses its meaning. If there is no real hope offered by the verse, or no instruction, why was it put in the Bible?

2) Restrict it.

Perhaps few parents succeed in training a child in the way he should go. Maybe we need to restrict our application of the verse to only applying to the parents who have *really* excelled with their children. It is possible that what we perceive as successful parenting is not really enough and that the parents who have "failed" never really fulfilled their obligation to train their children properly.

The problem with this approach is that even if we raise the bar on what it means to train a child in the way he should go, it still seems like there are exceptions. If we raise the bar even higher than that, the hope offered in the Bible seems unattainable. It would be like saying, "If you do a perfect job raising your child, and never falter, your child will follow all that you taught him." Do you see how that waters down the verse, just like redefining all the terms does? If you raise the standard to something that is unattainable, then what hope is there? Why try to meet the standard? And why even put the verse in the Bible?

3) Rethink it.

Perhaps it's not a promise at all, but a principle. Perhaps it's a guiding truth of life but not an outright guarantee. For example, the verse following Proverbs 22:6 says, "The rich rule over the poor."[11] It seems that this is a general truth. Not every rich person rules over poor people. Some rich people live as recluses, holed up in their homes, ruling over

[11] Proverbs 22:7a

no one. However, generally speaking, the rich do rule over the poor, and the poor end up serving the rich.

The problem with this approach is that the success rate of parents doesn't seem to even support the idea of it being a guiding truth. In other words, it not only doesn't seem like an "absolute promise" but it doesn't even seem like a truth that generally reflects life well.

So which is it? I think it is number 2 mixed in with a little number 3. I don't think it is an absolute guarantee that your child will follow you in every single area in which they've been taught. That would seem to go against the teaching of free will. However, Proverbs 22:6 was put in the Bible to give you hope—to inspire you to a certain course in your parenting. *Even if* it is only a guiding principle, then it is one that is worth following. Good parenting produces good results. That should be true in every case, or at least in the vast majority of the cases. That is the spirit of Proverbs 22:6, and if the hope we take from that verse gets any more watered down than that, we should seriously question whether we truly believe God's Word or not.

> *Proverbs 22:6 was put in the Bible to give you hope—to inspire you to a certain course in your parenting.*

I also believe that most parents do not adequately raise their children. Many take a whack at it, but few hit the nail on the head—and if you don't hit a nail squarely on the head, the nail doesn't usually fare well, does it? It is not enough to go to church, set a curfew, keep your kids out of R-rated movies, and keep them off drugs. Training a child in the way he should go involves a much deeper level of involvement than most parents pursue, and perhaps for which they are willing to sacrifice.

As parents, we can hold a high level of confidence in the outcome of our kids. Even if we don't have an absolute 100%-money-back-guarantee, we still have a principle given to us by God for the very purpose of giving us such a hope and expectation. Parent in a way that teaches your kids how to follow God wholeheartedly, and expect that to bear good and lasting fruit in the lives of your kids.

Remember that everything that does not come from faith is sin (Romans 14:23). God wants us to trust Him with this. Too many parents live in fear instead of faith. They fear that God's Word won't prove true, or that they will be the exception. Instead, we need to live in faith that if we trust in and follow His Word it will lead us down a good path. Have faith that God's way will win!

You Can Win

What would you think if God didn't allow someone to be a pastor because he was ugly or disfigured or because he had a brother who didn't follow the Lord? It would seem wrong to disallow someone from pastoring because of something that he had no control over, had nothing to do with his job, and had nothing to do with the set roles that God had given him.

So, you may be asking yourself, what does this have to do with parenting? My response is, "Everything!" Carefully look at the following verses:

1 Timothy 3:4,5 [An elder] must manage his own family well and see that his children obey him with proper

*respect. (If anyone does not know how to manage his
own family, how can he take care of God's church?)*

*1 Timothy 3:12 A deacon must be the husband of but
one wife and must manage his children and his household well.*

*Titus 1:6 An elder must be blameless, the husband of
but one wife, a man whose children believe and are
not open to the charge of being wild and disobedient.*

I personally think these are the strongest verses in the Bible
that definitively show that you can win with your kids. I can't
see any possible way to explain them away.

1 Timothy 3 and Titus 1 lay out the requirements for
church leaders, and one of the requirements is that they have
good kids—kids who are believers, who are not wild and disobedient, who are manageable, and who respect their fathers.
Now if a father has a fair amount of control of these things in
his kids' lives, then this requirement is fair. However, if fathers
really have little or no control over how their kids turn out,
then this requirement for church leadership is as random as
if God required His leaders to be Caucasian, or if God judged
them based on the behavior of their extended family. Do you
see the connection now? God would not require that leaders
have good kids if having good kids was merely a product of
dumb luck!

It's important to understand that there is no special parenting gift that God has given his leaders. They are just ordinary
people. If they can have good kids, anyone can have good kids
by applying the same principles. Having good kids is a result of
following God's principles in your life, and in your parenting
practices!

God believes that parents are equipped for, responsible for, and capable of producing godly kids—kids who are believers, who are not wild and disobedient, who are manageable, and who respect their parents. Parent, you *must* be convinced of this. You *must* take ownership for how your children turn out, and you *must* have faith that with God, all things are possible.[12]

Everyone else may think that your job as a parent is just to educate, provide for, and protect your kids until they are on their own. Everyone else may think that you just have to cross your fingers and hope they turn out okay, but you are not everyone else. You must lock into the responsibility that God has given you. He clearly states that you can change the outcome of your kids' lives. *Do you believe this?* How you answer this question will profoundly impact your parenting.

> God believes that parents are equipped for, responsible for, and capable of producing godly kids.

Worst Case Scenario

Sometimes when we see teens that are going through tough times it can be discouraging and we wonder if all our parenting efforts in the early years are really worth it. We've already looked at some reasons to believe that you can have a great deal of confidence in the fruit of your parenting. However, let's take a look at it from a little bit of a different angle now. Suppose you could see into the future and you knew that when your child hit 15 he would rebel. This could take many different forms, but suppose you knew that your teen would

[12] Philippians 4:13

do poorly in school, cheat on tests, participate in vandalism, swear profusely, not come home until four in the morning, if at all, and would refuse to go to church altogether. My guess is that we all know a teen or two that has gone through something like that—maybe a little better or maybe a little worse. I don't expect our kids to rebel at that level, but I've seen it enough that it troubles me, and in my times of doubt I wonder if that could happen in my family. The question I have is this: If I knew that my kids would rebel at 15, what would I do differently now?

Another way to look at it is this: at that level of rebelliousness you've lost most of your input into your kid's life. So I might ask myself: what would I want to pass on to my child to prepare him for life before I lose that place of influence?

I would want to make sure my child was educated enough to have a good paying job. I'd want him to be used to hard work so that he could handle the stress of the daily grind. If you can't provide for yourself in life, it can be hard to dig yourself out of a hole. I'd also want him to know some other basic life skills, like financial management.

I'd want him to know the dangers of premarital sex, drugs, and the abuse of alcohol.

If he knew at least 100 verses by heart, it would encourage me to know that God's Word was continually available to guide and direct my child, and to chip away at his conscience. (Actually, I'd say 500 verses, but I don't want to overwhelm you.) I'd also hope he would have a wealth of past sermons, Sunday school lessons, and teachings from his parents that the Holy Spirit could bring to his mind at the appropriate time.

I'd want him to know the principles that a man reaps what he sows,[13] and if you sow the wind you reap the whirlwind.[14] I'd want him to know that a good life is found when we pursue

[13] Galatians 6:7
[14] Hosea 8:7

God's will. If you sow good choices, you reap a good life.

It would be extremely important to me that he knew he was loved by his God, his parents, and his family. Although he could run from many things, I'd want that to always haunt him (in a sense) and to continually be a pull on his heart. I'd want him to know that, like they were for the prodigal son,[15] forgiveness and restoration are always close at hand.

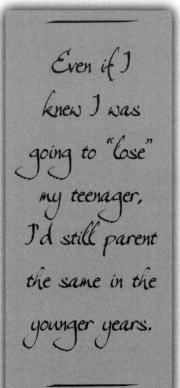

Even if I knew I was going to "lose" my teenager, I'd still parent the same in the younger years.

These are a few of the things that come to my mind. I'd want to do everything within my power to equip my child for his time of rebelliousness in hopes that it would be short-lived and not too destructive. That would take a large amount of energy and time, but in the end, hopefully, it would all be worthwhile to save my child.

Interestingly enough, when you think about it, that level of parenting is the same level I'd recommend to someone who wants to raise a champion for Christ. Even if I knew I was going to "lose" my teenager, I'd still parent the same in the younger years. So maybe all this fear related to losing our children is just a distraction from the task at hand. I don't know the future. I don't know how my kids or your kids will turn out. I have certain hopes and expectations for the future, but those may be somewhat irrelevant. I do know for certain what God has called me to today, and I need to be faithful with that instead of frozen in the fear of the unknown.

Stay the course, Parent!

[15] Luke 15:11-32

God Is for You

The Old Testament wraps up with an interesting verse:

Malachi 4:6 "He will turn the hearts of the fathers to their children, and the hearts of the children to their fathers; or else I will come and strike the land with a curse."

In some ways this is a difficult passage. It is a prophecy referring to the coming of John the Baptist in the spirit and power of Elijah.[16] It would be interesting to discuss why the Old Testament ends this way, and equally as interesting to try to discover why and how John's ministry was characterized by the impact on fathers and sons. Instead of focusing on these intriguing questions, I'd like to focus on something that the passage much more clearly communicates: namely, that God cares about parenting.

God was concerned that fathers' hearts were not given to their children, and He was equally concerned that the children's hearts were not given to their fathers. Evidently, this was so troubling to God that He decided to send a prophet for the express purpose of addressing this concern, or so it seems from this verse. Obviously, there was more to John's mission than that, but this issue was certainly a central part of his mission. Not only was it on God's heart, but He said that if this prophet failed to turn the hearts of fathers and sons, He would strike the land with a curse. He meant serious business.

Again, it would be an interesting discussion as to whether or not John the Baptist fulfilled this part of his mission. If not, were we somehow cursed as a result? I don't have the answers to these questions, but I can tell this much about Malachi 4:6:

---

[16] Luke 1:17; Matthew 11:14; 17:11-12

parenting is important to God. Since parenting is important to God, you can be assured that God is in complete support of your efforts to become a better parent.

Another passage that shows that God is in support of your parenting is the passage about the shepherd that leaves the ninety-nine sheep to go after the one that strays away. My guess is that some people will think this is a misinterpretation on my part, as we don't typically think of this passage in this way. However, the illustration of the lost sheep is given twice, and makes two different points.

When the account is given in Luke 15, it is given in the context of the lost coin and the lost son (or the prodigal son), and it starts off by mentioning that the Pharisees were grumbling about Jesus ministering to sinful people. In context it is clearly talking about God's concern for even one lost soul, and this is how most people normally think of the parable.

However, the exact same illustration is also given in Matthew 18. Here, it is clearly in the midst of a different sermon, and Jesus' point is completely different. It's about children.

Matthew 18:10 "See that you do not look down on one of these little ones. For I tell you that their angels in heaven always see the face of my Father in heaven."

Let's stop here for a moment. Who are "these little ones?" Are they lost people, or are they children? I can't think of any other place that non-Christians are referred to as "little ones" and the chapter begins with Jesus pulling a child to Himself and saying that we need to become like one of these "little ones." So it is clear from the context that Jesus is still talking about children. Let's continue with the rest of the passage:

Matthew 18:12-14 "What do you think? If a man owns a hundred sheep, and one of them wanders away, will he not leave the ninety-nine on the hills and go to look for the one that wandered off? And if he finds it, I tell you the truth, he is happier about that one sheep than about the ninety-nine that did not wander off. In the same way your Father in heaven is not willing that any of these little ones should be lost."

Clearly the "little ones" in verse 14 are the same "little ones" from verse 10, who are the same "little ones" from verse 6. The New Century Version states it plainly:

Matthew 18:14 In the same way, your Father in heaven does not want any of these little children to be lost. (NCV)

God's desire is that we would not lose a single one of our children. Not a single one out of our families, and not a single one out of our churches. The *Guinness Book of Records* lists the wife of Reodor Vassilyev as having given birth to 69 children in the 1700's. I have a hard time believing it too, but it also says another couple had their 55th child in 1951, so I suppose it is possible. (After all, if you can have 55, what's another 14?) That's a lot of mouths to feed and bottoms to diaper! That's also a great amount of love, discipline, and instruction that needs to be given. It seems like it would be easy

> God's desire is that we would not lose a single one of our children. Not a single one out of our families, and not a single one out of our churches.

with that many children to let one fall through the cracks. If I had 69 kids and one turned away from the Lord, as hard as that would be, I might still be tempted to feel pretty good about saving the other 68. But God's desire is that not one would be lost—not a single one.

It says that He is "not willing that any of these little ones should be lost." Several translations put it as, "It is not the will of your father." It is not God's will that we should lose one. It is against His will. God is opposed to it. He is 100% for your family, and 100% against you losing your children. This is a clear point He is making in this passage, and I am intentionally belaboring it. No parent is okay with losing a single child, and neither is God.

If God feels so strongly about not losing children, it stands to reason that God is supportive of your work as a parent. We know that God is not willing that one would be lost, and from Malachi 2:15 we know that He desires godly offspring. If this is His desire, then certainly God will give you wisdom, strength, and courage that you desperately need in order to win in parenting.

This doesn't mean that effort is not required on our part. We know better than that. But neither does it mean that it all depends on us. God is at work in us, through us, and for our children.

Here's another verse that talks about God's will:

1 John 5:14-15 This is the confidence we have in approaching God: that if we ask anything according to His will, He hears us. And if we know that He hears us — whatever we ask — we know that we have what we asked of Him.

I don't mean to use this verse as an oversimplification of the parenting process, as if you can just say the magic words and automatically win with your kids. And I don't intend to offer false hope. However, there is a ton of hope offered here. It is certainly fair to say that God loves to answer prayers that are in line with His will. We already saw that God's will is that not one of your children would be lost, so we can say with confidence that God loves answering your prayers regarding the winning of your children's hearts.

Parenting is certainly a formidable and daunting task, but there should also be great comfort in realizing that God is for you, and He desires the same things you do in the salvation and successful upbringing of your children!

A final verse to ponder:

Hebrews 13:20-21 May the God of peace, who through the blood of the eternal covenant brought back from the dead our Lord Jesus, that great Shepherd of the sheep, equip you with everything good for doing His will, and may He work in us what is pleasing to Him, through Jesus Christ, to whom be glory for ever and ever. Amen.

Making Sense of the Prodigal

When a child grows up and strays from God, whose fault is it? Is it the fault of the parents for failing to train the child properly, or is it the fault of the child for rebelling? This is a sensitive issue that requires careful handling.

The danger of saying that it is no fault of the parent is that it discourages parents because it implies that their efforts make no difference. If your parenting makes a difference, you should have to answer for how you did with what God entrusted to you. We will discover that God does, in fact, hold us accountable as parents.

On the other hand, it would seem unfair to blame all the choices of a grown prodigal on his parents. Taking this approach often puts undue shame on parents. We need to be careful to not put more responsibility on parents than God does. We cannot hold parents responsible for every wrong choice their grown children make. At some point our children are old enough to be on their own, and the choices they make are theirs and theirs alone. Consider the following:

Ezekiel 18:14-20 "But suppose this son has a son who sees all the sins his father commits, and though he sees them, he does not do such things:

"He does not eat at the mountain shrines or look to the idols of the house of Israel. He does not defile his neighbor's wife. He does not oppress anyone or require a pledge for a loan. He does not commit robbery but gives his food to the hungry and provides clothing for the naked. He withholds his hand from sin and takes no usury or excessive interest. He keeps my laws and follows my decrees.

"He will not die for his father's sin; he will surely live. But his father will die for his own sin, because he practiced extortion, robbed his brother and did what was wrong among his people.

"Yet you ask, 'Why does the son not share the guilt of his father?' Since the son has done what is just and right and has been careful to keep all my decrees, he will surely live. The soul who sins is the one who will die. The son will not share the guilt of the father, nor

will the father share the guilt of the son. The righteousness of the righteous man will be credited to him, and the wickedness of the wicked will be charged against him."

Take careful note that in verse 20 it says, "The son will not share the guilt of the father, nor will the father share the guilt of the son." Parents will not be held accountable for the actions of their grown children.

However, that does not relieve all parental responsibility. In the chapter on discipline we will look at how God held Eli responsible for his parenting. While he was not technically held responsible for his sons' sin, he was held responsible for his own sin in failing to restrain them.

So, whose fault is it when a grown child turns away from the pattern of his upbringing? That is an interesting question that I have wrestled over as I have watched families struggle. I've finally concluded that this is not my issue with which to wrestle. God will sort out who is responsible for what. I need only concern myself with *my* parenting and *my* kids.

Psalms 131:1 O Lord, my heart is not proud, nor my eyes haughty; nor do I involve myself in great matters, or in things too difficult for me. (NAS)

I am going to parent with the belief that parenting makes a huge difference, that God wants us to win, and that winning is attainable and expected. I choose this path of emphasis, because it is the biblical emphasis. God does *not* say, "Train a child in the way he should go, and when he is old he will not turn from it...but if he doesn't don't worry about it, that is out of your hands." In Proverbs 22:6 the emphasis clearly rests on the premise that you can and should win with your kids. Again, God does *not* say, "An elder must be blameless, the husband of but one wife, a man whose children believe and are not open to the charge of being wild and disobedient...but if he's got one or two rebels in his house don't worry about that, after all, kids do have free will." Instead, in Titus 1:6 the emphasis is that parents can win with their kids.

If one of my children struggles, I will repent for whatever mistakes I have made. As I mentioned earlier, I am not a perfect parent. We have all made mistakes. I trust that somehow, someway, God is true to His word, and His plan will prevail.

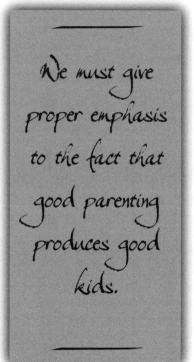

We must give proper emphasis to the fact that good parenting produces good kids.

I will move on with my life, not burdened by guilt, but living in the shadow of His grace.

In viewing rebels in other families, I try to be careful not to judge the parents who have tried hard but whose children have turned from God. To parents of grown prodigals I offer my condolences. I'm sure they have already beaten themselves up a thousand times for mistakes they have made. I would have no basis to critique their parenting of their own children unless they had somehow lived in extreme indifference to God's Word. Otherwise, their responsibility with their own families is between them and God.

I think that in Christianity we tend to emphasize the possibility that there could be exceptions because we don't want to hurt anyone's feelings. I don't want to hurt anyone's feelings either. My heart breaks for parents whose kids have struggled. However, we must give proper emphasis to the fact that good parenting produces good kids, because that is what God stresses in His Word. That should encourage and inspire us to parent with stout hearts.

– 3 –
Winning Ways

If I had to boil down parenting to a few key topics, they would be love, discipline, and training. That is why each of these topics merits its own chapter. Of course, if we boil it down to just these three, we lose some of the flavor of the Christian home. This chapter captures some of the other important aspects of parenting—the seasoning, if you will.

> The way these kids were treated in their formative years shaped their personalities, mental abilities, and every aspect of their futures.

Get Them While They Are Young

*Ere a child has reached to seven
Teach him all the way to heaven;
Better still the work will thrive If
he learns before he's five.*
— *Charles H. Spurgeon*

While there is hope for a child (or adult) of any age, let's not get fooled into thinking that age makes no difference. Fifty-year-olds can change, as can twenty year olds, but the potential for change in a toddler is limitless. Little ones are fresh slates. Every thing you say and do, every expression of love, and every interaction with a child shapes who he will become.

Kathleen and I once watched a documentary on kids who had been abandoned in childhood. They were left in their cribs in orphanages, abandoned, and even raised by animals. It was a heartbreaking story, but the thing that amazed me was that some of the kids *never* learned how to interact with people or to even talk. I would have believed that such neglect would slow the learning process, but I never would have thought it would be so incredibly detrimental. The way these kids were treated in their formative years shaped their personalities, mental abilities, and every aspect of their futures.

George Barna has done much research on people's basic belief systems. He says that most people's worldview is set by the time they are just nine-years-old.[17] What they believe at that age about God, Jesus, the Bible, and eternal life is likely to be what they will believe for the rest of their lives! Kids are imprinted dramatically in the early years.

There is a bush in my yard that is about eight feet tall, which is about six too many. I suppose it has been there since my house was built over 50 years ago. It is gnarly and twisted and strong enough that I can easily climb in it and on it. If it wasn't prickly it would make an excellent fort for the kids to play under. But it is just too big. It's a monstrosity. I try to trim it, but I can only knock a foot or so off the top without doing some major chain-sawing and risking killing it (which is not a bad idea). I wish the previous owners had trimmed it when it was younger and smaller, because now it is very hard to manage.

The same is true of people. They typically can be impacted the most when they are young. If you wait until they are thirteen or fourteen to teach them, you have lost much valuable time, and may have lost their hearts. In other words, their hearts are prone to be more drawn to you than to the attractions of the world when they are little. When you lose this spot in their lives you lose a considerable amount of influence.

I do think many parents unnecessarily lose their kids in the teen years. Parenting in the teen years is important, but

[17] George Barna, *Transforming Children into Spiritual Champions*, pg. 47, Ventura, CA: Regal, ©2003

parenting in the teen years is going to be one hundred times more difficult if you haven't parented well in the early years. That's why this book focuses on the preteen years. If you have older kids, I believe God's principles can still dramatically impact your home. However, if you still have little children, it is critical to do all that you can now, while their hearts are still so receptive to being shaped.

Putting it into Action

A young boy was fishing in the old fishing hole. He had a piece of grass hanging from his mouth, a straw hat resting over his eyebrows, and he was leaning back against a tree. His pole was propped up next to him as he listened to the sounds of frogs croaking all around him. An old timer sauntered by and interrupted, "Any luck today son?"

"No sir, the fish just aren't biting today. I fish just as much as everyone else, but it seems like I never catch anything. It's just not fair."

"Lemme see whatcha got goin' today," the old timer intruded as he grabbed the pole and reeled it in. The boy sat up and watched as the old timer discovered that there wasn't any bait on the hook. In fact there wasn't even a hook, just a bobber.

"Son, you lost your hook. That explain' your poor luck. Lemme help." He took one of his own hooks, and tied it to the boy's line. Then he asked the boy for a worm, and the boy said he was out. He took out one of his own worms and put it on the hook, and even left a few worms for the boy saying, "Here ya go son, this'll fix ya up. Have fun now!"

The lad gratefully replied "Thank you sir. That's mighty kind of you," and he returned to his lazy afternoon pastime.

A week later the scene repeated itself. The same old timer happened by the boy and said, "Son, you havin' any luck today?"

"No sir," replied the boy. "Fishing just never seems to work for me. I sit out here for hours on end and I hardly ever even get a bite."

"Lemme see whatcha got goin' today," he said as he pulled in the boy's line while the boy continued to complain. To his astonishment, once again, there was no bait and no hook. "Son, you ain't goin' to catch nothin' without some bait and a hook."

"Yes sir."

"So whatcha doin' son?"

"Sir, after you helped me the other day I caught a snag and I lost my bait and hook. I've been meaning to fix it up, but I just haven't gotten around to it. Besides that, I never really cared much for sticking those worms on the hook anyhow."

The old timer said, "Okay then," and started shuffling down the path, "but ya ain't never gonna catch nothin' without some bait and a hook."

Many parents are like this young fisherman. They know what changes need to take place in their home, but they don't want to make the hard choices that will bring those changes. They want to enjoy the benefits of parenting, without embracing the work that comes with it. Their goals are not necessarily to accomplish anything specific, but just to try to enjoy the ride and to do things their own way.

Let me ask you a couple of questions:

What does your child need from you that you are not giving him or her?

What areas in your parenting do you sense that God wants you to change but you are reluctant to do so?

Chances are good that most people will answer these questions fairly accurately. In other words, you may already know what you need to know. You don't need to be told what to do; you just need to apply what you already know.

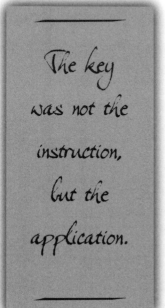

The key was not the instruction, but the application.

Sometimes we need encouragement more than we need knowledge. I recently listened to a CD of *another* sermon on prayer. I knew I wasn't praying like I should, especially as a pastor. I didn't need more knowledge or information about prayer; I just needed to pray more. I did end up making some significant changes, but the growth in my life didn't come from listening to another sermon. It came from making some difficult choices. The sermons were encouraging to me, but the key was not the *instruction*, but the *application*.

As we strive to grow as parents, it is too easy to get caught up learning instead of doing. As you think, read, and learn about parenting, always go back to application. Always ask yourself, "What changes does God want me to make in my parenting?"

The Bible clearly calls us to application. Always remember the following verse:

James 1:22 Do not merely listen to the word, and so deceive yourselves. Do what it says.

Passing the Life-baton

We've all heard numerous illustrations of what will really matter to you at the end of your life. At that time you won't care nearly as much about promotions, titles, and having a clean house. What will matter is how you've followed God and the legacy you've left behind—not that you've got trophies and awards to document your successes, but that you've loved other people and touched their lives.

2 Corinthians 3:2,3 "You yourselves are our letter, written on our hearts, known and read by everybody. You show that you are a letter from Christ, the result of our ministry, written not with ink but with the Spirit of the living God, not on tablets of stone but on tablets of human hearts."

Paul realized that the impact of his life left a legacy. The love he showed people left a mark on people's hearts. Somehow they were permanently changed—by God, and through Paul. I'd like to leave a legacy like that on people's hearts. I want my life to expand God's kingdom and to touch the lives of others.

While I realize and value the significance of this outside my family, I can't imagine having any greater impact than the mark I will leave on my own kids. My children will be my most enduring letter to the world.

I absolutely love the movie *Pistol Pete*. It chronicles the true story of eighth-grader Pete Marovich and the struggles he faced being a misfit basketball prodigy on a high school team. I love how the movie captured the vision of Pete's dad, both as a parent and as a ball player. Although he was a respectable basketball player himself, he passed the vision of his life on to his son, who in turn helped take basketball to a new level. Pete's dad played ball with him, gave him drills, talked to him about strategy, worked to instill confidence in him, stood up for him, and believed in him. Pete went on to become college basketball's highest scorer of all time.

> *Children will invariably talk, eat, walk, think, respond, and act like their parents. Give them a target to shoot at...*

Psalms 45:16 Your sons will take the place of your fathers; you will make them princes throughout the land.

Some day our children will take our place. I've learned countless lessons in life. I've made many mistakes, and I've learned how to avoid a few. My understanding of God's grace, mercy, and holiness has grown immensely. I don't want to just let that all end with me and have my children start from scratch. Instead, as much as possible, I want my kids to take my place. I want to pass the life-baton to them.

At the end of my life, that will be a major part of what counts. Though I may not excel in numerous other areas in life, my desire is to parent in a way that leaves no regrets. Few griefs will outweigh seeing them drop the baton, and few joys will overshadow seeing them continue in the race.

"Oh God, be merciful to my family. Help me run the race well, and help my children to continue the race and to run hard for you. At the end of my children's

lives may it be said of them that they fought the good fight, finished the race, and kept the faith.[18] May all of our lives glorify you."

Setting an Example

Philippians 1:27a Whatever happens, conduct yourselves in a manner worthy of the gospel of Christ.

I remember walking into an indoor flea market with my dad when I was a young man. My eyes were soon drawn to a picture of a scantily dressed woman. The picture was placed such that I doubted that any male could possibly fail to notice its existence on his way out the door. I suppose I was looking for some validation that my own temptations or failures in that area were normal, but for whatever reason, I decided to put my dad to the test.

Dad was a godly man, a deacon in the church, and always upright as near as I could tell, but I really wanted to see how he would face this temptation. A few minutes later we headed back out of the

... Give them a goal to work toward. Give them a pattern that they can see clearly, and you give them something that gold and silver cannot buy.

— Billy Graham

[18] 2 Timothy 4:7

store, and I fixed my eyes not on the painting, but on Dad. What would he do? He certainly would notice the painting, but would he do a double-take? Although I'm sure dad had his struggles at times, he passed this particular test—and that test is the one that mattered to me. Dad passed away over a dozen years ago and he never knew this story. He never knew my struggles; and he never knew the example he set for me. In the same way, I may never know when my kids will be watching me to see just how my Christianity is lived out in real life. When that time comes, I hope to be the man of God who lives in a manner worthy of my Lord. Of course, to pass that test I will need to be a man of integrity, a man who chooses correctly not just when watched by others, but a man who daily and faithfully lives in a manner worthy of my Lord.

FROM OUR HOME

Imitators

Ephesians 5:1,2a Be imitators of God, therefore, as dearly loved children and live a life of love.

As I hopped into the car one day I coughed three times. My first son, who was about 18-months-old at the time, was in his car seat next to me and he also coughed three times. I looked at him to see if he was teasing me, but he didn't seem to be paying any attention. Just to make sure, I proceeded to cough two times. He coughed two times. I coughed one time and he coughed one time. I smiled at him and messed up his hair and drove off.

I was struck by the fact that he was watching me so closely that he was subconsciously imitating even the littlest things I did. What other things is he imitating? That's fine with me if he coughs when I cough, but what bad habits is he learning from me? For a long time we wondered why he so easily learned to say "thank you", but it seemed that no amount of training could get him to say "please." Finally my wife and I realized that in both cases he was just imitating us. In one case for the better and in the other for the worse. Parenting is scary!

I also started to wonder who else was imitating me. I don't particularly want people to imitate me, but if they do, I hope it will be for the better and not for the worse. I wish I lived such an example of the Christian life that I could say like Paul, "Follow my example as I follow the example of Christ."[19] But the scary thing is that others may follow my example whether I tell them to or not.

Lastly, I had to ask myself who I was imitating. Like my son imitates his daddy, I want to imitate my heavenly Father. I need to be so close to Him that if He coughs I will cough.

Parenting under Pressure

I know what some of you are thinking by now. As Charlie Brown would say, "Aargh!" I'm sorry if you feel like your cork is about ready to pop. We've already covered a lot of topics, and you may feel the pressure building up. Most parents already feel like they are doing a bad job at parenting. Parental guilt is known to most of us, and a book like this could easily serve to point out even more areas that you need to improve in. Instead of offering hope it could make you feel hopeless.

Our parenting methods and involvement have undoubtedly evolved over time. If someone had told us five years ago that

[19] 1 Corinthians 11:1

we needed to do everything we are currently doing, we would have rolled our eyes and shook our heads. Yet over time God had led us down a path we never would have thought we could have handled just a few years ago.

Don't get overwhelmed. Implement what you can and see how it goes. Keep striving to improve and apply more ideas as God leads. God does not want to overwhelm you (and neither do I). He wants to help you grow and win with your family.

Take comfort in this verse:

Isaiah 41:10 So do not fear, for I am with you; do not be dismayed, for I am your God. I will strengthen you and help you; I will uphold you with my righteous right hand.

Humbling Ourselves to a Noble Call

Like everyone else, I struggle with doing what I should. Usually this is because I'd rather do something else. I really despise doing yard work, but I suppose if there was nothing in the world that was more pleasurable, then yard work wouldn't seem like such a bad thing. Yet life is not like that, is it? Life is full of choices. I can do yard work, or I can watch football. I can do what I need to do or what I want to do, and it only takes a casual glimpse at my poor lawn to know which priority usually wins in my house.

Hopefully the same can't be said of my choices concerning my kids. I try to make the right choices when it comes to loving, training, and disciplining them as I should. Sure, there are distractions and responsibilities that tug at my heart, but I try to be careful to prioritize my family. It's a tough balance isn't it?

Jesus had a hard choice to make. He was so distressed over going to the cross that He was wrestling with God in prayer, pleading for a different way, and sweating drops of blood in His anguish.[20] Yet He chose the cross and, in doing so, paid for our sins and provided forgiveness to all who would put their faith in Him. How did He make such a difficult choice?

> *Philippians 2:5-8 "Your attitude should be the same as that of Christ Jesus: who, being in very nature God, did not consider equality with God something to be grasped, but made Himself nothing, taking the very nature of a servant, being made in human likeness. And being found in appearance as a man, He* humbled Himself *and became obedient to death – even death on a cross!"*

Jesus chose the cross because He humbled Himself. He yielded His will to the will of His Father. Although He had every right to annihilate all of us rather than die for us, He laid down that right. He gladly chose to die to His own rights and let the rights of His Father win out.

We wrestle with our rights as well, don't we? Don't I have the right to a career, to enjoy some alone time with my spouse, and to a good night's sleep? Shouldn't I be able to enjoy doing a few of the things that I really like to do? Is a day off, a true day of rest, too much to ask?

I don't know if I really have any of those "rights", but in some ways it is irrelevant now. As a parent of six, those "rights" are rarely realized. Instead, I've learned to find joy in following a higher call on my life.

In a casual conversation a few years back someone asked me, "What do you do in your free-time?"

I pondered the question for a moment and said, "I think I'm out of that phase in my life." Seriously. There is little free-time for me or my wife. With six little ones how can there be?

---

[20] Luke 22:44; Hebrews 12:4

I know that some will say that is unhealthy, but let's get real here. With a church, a wife, and six kids, that pretty much uses up all of my free-time, don't you think?

There really is no such thing as free-time. It is all God-time. There is time in which God allows us to rest, relax, enjoy life, and read a book, but it is not free. It is His. We need to surrender our "rights" to do what we want. The above verse says that we should take on the attitude of Christ Jesus. We need to humble ourselves under God's plan for our daily choices, time, and lives.

> *There is time in which God allows us to rest, relax, enjoy life, and read a book, but it is not free. It is His.*

In speaking of His own life, Jesus said, "I tell you the truth, unless a kernel of wheat falls to the ground and dies, it remains only a single seed. But if it dies, it produces many seeds" (John 12:24).

This is a powerful principle. As I hold onto my "rights", very little fruit is produced in my life. More football gets watched, more video games get played, and more mountains get climbed, but little fruit is produced. It is as I willingly die to those "rights," or die to myself, that my life produces the fruit of a good family and a growing church.

In parenting we need to stop mourning what we've lost because we are parents. Sure, good parenting comes at a cost, but do you focus only on what you've lost, or do you also focus on what you are gaining? If the death of my own dreams means the flourishing of my children, should I mourn the wilting of my own life, or rejoice in the budding of my children's lives?

Psalms 144:12 "Then our sons in their youth will be like well-nurtured plants, and our daughters will be like pillars carved to adorn a palace."

In humility, Jesus yielded to the Father's desires, and it produced life for us. In the same way, as we yield to the Father's will in our parenting, it will produce fruit in our children. God's work in them will make them spiritually strong, healthy, and beautiful. Seeing those dreams fulfilled is far more valuable to me than the memory of watching a last minute victory, or building a name for myself. That is what makes the entire process not one of drudgery, but a wonderful and exciting journey. Just as Jesus went to the cross "for the joy set before Him,"[21] let us also, for the joy set before us, humbly accept God's noble call on our lives.

Parenting with Purpose

"The Christians who have turned the world upside down have been men and women with a vision in their hearts and the Bible in their hands."
—T.B. Maston

If the death of my own dreams means the flourishing of my children, should I mourn the wilting of my own life, or rejoice in the budding of my children's lives?

[21] Hebrews 12:3

Our church has done a sports camp for several years now. There is nothing like watching your little kids play a game of competitive soccer. With absolutely zero drive and negligible skill, they charge the field with only one thing in mind: when will this game end so we can have some popsicles? Somehow they just don't seem to grasp the importance of kicking a ball into a net more often than the other side kicks the ball into the other net. They stare off into space, chase butterflies, chat with each other, and tie their shoes at the worst possible times.

It is easy to approach parenting with this same passivity. I don't mean to say that we don't care—we just don't have our heads in the game. Each day can seem mundane instead of strategic. We lose track of time and a sense of urgency that we haven't a minute to lose. The things that are most important to us start to get the least amount of attention. Instead of being a significant focal point of our service to God, parenting becomes something that we squeeze in amongst a hundred other tasks.

Paul did not live life that way. He understood that as Christians we have purpose in life, and he lived his life with that purpose in mind. Focused. Deliberate. Passionate.

> *Instead of being a significant focal point of our service to God, parenting becomes something that we squeeze in amongst a hundred other tasks.*

1 Corinthians 9:26 So I do not run without a goal. I fight like a boxer who is hitting something — not just the air. (NCV)

Paul understood that his goal was to win as many people for Christ as he could by wholeheartedly sharing his faith. This was not a unique purpose of Paul's but one that all Christians share. That includes you and I *and* our children.

Our children are also created with purpose.

Ephesians 2:10 For we are God's workmanship, created in Christ Jesus to do good works, which God prepared in advance for us to do.

Before birth, God gave thought to each child and the purposes He would have them fulfill, and He lovingly created each individual with that intent in mind.

Since we are created with purpose, we should live life purposefully. Given that our children are created with purpose, we should also build into them purposefully. Our parenting must not be half-hearted or directionless; instead, we need to be visionary! Like Paul, we need to keep our heads in the game.

Keep the End Product in Mind

Ephesians 5:1 Be imitators of God, therefore, as dearly loved children

Earlier we looked at some of the goals of parenting. It is an important enough topic that it is worth another look. What is the end result of our parenting? It is to produce an 18-year-old man or woman who is godly. Each child should have the character of a godly man or woman as described in the Bible.

Although I can't predict exactly how each kid will turn out and how their individual personalities will affect them, I still at times will try to picture what I'd like to see in each child when he or she is 17 or 18. I'd like to have children who are polite, who converse well with others, who are capable of leading others and being role models. I picture them sharing the gospel with their friends, being well-liked by their peers, and being willing and eager to sit and eat lunch in the high school cafeteria with those who don't quite fit in. I hope they'll be excited about their futures and that they'll be eager to go into careers where they can serve and influence others. I expect them to be kids who are loved by their teachers and coaches. I expect them to be equipped to handle disappointments, let downs, and losses. Of course I expect them to make mistakes, and I hope they'll be able to handle those as well, because they will make mistakes for the rest of their lives.

I'm not just measuring them against some Joe Christian figure in my head; I'm trying to help them to become more and more like Jesus. The characteristics I just described are how I imagine a Christ-like life would look in the life of a young man (except of course without the sin part).

Many parents aim too low. They just want their kids to be decent people – good citizens. Christians should want more. We should want our children to be model Christians, godly men and women, and influencers—men and women who imitate God, not their peers.

Luke 2:42-48 When He was twelve years old... they found Him in the temple courts, sitting among the teachers, listening to them and asking them questions. Everyone who heard Him was amazed at His understanding and His answers.

Jesus was an impressive young man at the age of twelve. Is

there any reason our kids can't be the same? We have all kinds of tools available to us: Christian books, videos, the Bible on tape, etc... Our kids can have a vast understanding of the Bible by the age of 12. I think they should know more than most adults, not only in relation to knowing the stories, but even in regards to wisdom and discernment.

We all know that the teen years can be particularly difficult. How encouraging it would be if much of our work was done by 12, and if the next 6 years could be spent on fine-tuning character areas and equipping them with ministry skills!

If we have our goal in mind, and if that goal is set as high as it should be, then that should help drive our day-to-day involvement in our kids' lives.

Critical Involvement

Please take a moment to take the following quiz:

1) Which parent has primary responsibility for bringing children up in the training and instruction of the Lord?

2) Which parent is responsible for managing the family?

3) Which parent should ensure that children are obedient and respectful?

4) Which parent has primary responsibility for child discipline?

You may be shocked to learn that it is the dad who is primarily responsible in each of these areas. I don't mean to downplay the role of moms at all. Let's face it: in most homes the moms are far more involved with the kids. They spend more time with them, care for them, cook for them, get up with them, and all kinds of other things. Moms are irreplaceable. But dads, you must stay involved! While you may not spend as many hours with the children, you must not disconnect or be a neutral party when it comes to parenting. You should be the driving force behind what your family does—the visionary. God sees you as such. Read each of the quiz questions again and then read the corresponding verse below. How would you say God sees your role, dad?

1) Which parent has primary responsibility for bringing children up in the training and instruction of the Lord?

Ephesians 6:4 <u>Fathers,</u> do not exasperate your children; instead, <u>bring them up in the training and instruction of the Lord.</u>

2 & 3) Which parent is responsible for managing the family? Which parent should ensure that children are obedient and respectful?

1 Timothy 3:4,5 <u>He</u> must <u>manage</u> his own family well and <u>see that his children obey him with proper respect.</u> (If anyone does not know how to manage his own family, how can he take care of God's church?)

4) Which parent has primary responsibility for child discipline?

Hebrews 12:9,10 Moreover, we have all had human <u>fathers who disciplined</u> us and we respected them for it. How much more should we submit to the Father of our spirits and live! <u>Our fathers disciplined us</u> for a

*little while as they thought best; but God disciplines
us for our good, that we may share in His holiness.*

In a Dilbert comic strip written by Scott Adams the following exchange took place:

Employee: Do you mind if I leave early to spend some time with my kids?
Exasperated boss: I never spent time with my kids and they turned out just fine!
Employee: How many do you have?
Boss: Threeish.

I met a father once who was reflecting on his job as a parent and said, "I think I did a good job with my kids. I went to all of their games."

Dads! That will not cut it. *We* cannot bring home the bacon and leave the child-raising to the moms. *We* cannot consider game attendance the fulfillment of our parental role. *We* cannot manage their lives from the office. *We* must be involved. *We* must know where our kids are, and I'm not talking about their physical location. *We* must know where they are in regard to character and spiritual development. *We* must know where they are going, and we must know how to help get them there. And *we* must help our spouses implement the plans that will help our kids grow. That's a lot of "we's", isn't it? But much of it is about "us." We dads need to step up to our God-given calling. God wants us involved, and our wives and kids need us to be involved.

To you moms out there without husbands or with disconnected husbands, I want to say I admire what you do. You have guts. You are pulling double duty to the best of your ability, and I believe that God will bless you in that. Keep up the good work!

Sacrificing for Your Children

1 John 3:16 This is how we know what love is: Jesus Christ laid down His life for us. And we ought to lay down our lives for our brothers.

> "I make a lot of money and I've given a lot of it to charities, but I've given all of myself to my wife and the kids, and that's the best donation I'll ever make."
> — Bill Cosby

During a preseason game between the Denver Broncos and the Arizona Cardinals, Shannon Sharpe was interviewed briefly. Shannon was formerly a tight end for the Broncos and holds many of the records for both the Broncos and the NFL for his position. Shannon said, "I may not have been the best friend, or the best son, or the best father, but I *was* the best football player." (That may not be an exact quote, but I think it is pretty close.)

I'm sure you have to sacrifice in many ways to be the best at football or at any sport. Some people sacrifice to be the best CEO or employee. Some things can be sacrificed: sleep, leisure time, partying, and eating whatever we feel like. Being disciplined with our lives is a good thing. However, some things must not be sacrificed, like God, marriage, and children.

I like Shannon. He was a great athlete and a lively character.

He's fun to watch on the field and fun to listen to off it. However, sacrificing your children to be the best at football is not something to boast about; it is something to weep over.

To be fair, I have no idea what kind of father he really is. Hopefully he was just exaggerating his commitment to football. In any case, Shannon Sharpe's accomplishments will not be remembered or cared about by many in 20 years. In contrast, in twenty years Shannon Sharpe's children will still care deeply about what kind of father they had. In 100 years no one will care about his athletic accomplishments. In 100 years his parenting will have impacted his children's children through several generations. If he truly laid his life down for football and sacrificed his children for his own glory, that would be the gravest mistake of his life.

A few days after Sharpe's comments there was a story in the newspaper about the standoff in Beslan, Russia. Chechnyan commandos stormed a school there and were holding hundreds of children and adults captive. Twenty-six women and children were released, but one of those women went back in to be with her children who were still captive. The standoff finally ended after a bloody shootout. I don't know what happened to that mother, but I know she willingly risked her own life for her children. She sacrificed her own life to comfort and protect her children.

We all give our lives to something. Each day our lives are spent and that day is over and gone, never to be spent again. Will we lay our lives down for our God? Our families? Our lost neighbors? For things that are on God's heart? We can't do much about the days that are gone, but how will our remaining days be spent?

When it comes to parenting, we love our kids, but we need to see that love translate into sacrifice, not *of* them, but *for* them. We sacrifice for them financially, physically, emotionally, and aromatically (think diapers). We sacrifice by choosing, not what is best for ourselves, but what is best for them when it comes to careers and pastimes. Anyone who has ever played mindless children's board games as an adult has sacrificed immensely for his child. And sleep? Boy do we sacrifice! It is normal and healthy to sacrifice for those we love.

As the verse above says, we should willingly lay down our lives for others. This is especially important within our families. This sacrificial attitude is the kind of love Christ demonstrated to us and calls us to show toward others. The result of living a life of sacrifice is not self-deprecation. Instead, it is a life of blessing and joy.

Acts 20:35 "In everything I did, I showed you that by this kind of hard work we must help the weak, remembering the words the Lord Jesus himself said: 'It is more <u>blessed</u> to give than to receive.'"

3 John 4 I have no greater joy than to hear that my children are walking in the truth.

FROM OUR HOME

Mr. Mom

Kathleen drove back to Iowa to see her mom shortly before her mom passed away. Here is an account of my experience that I wrote several days after she left:

I really haven't tried to do much pastoral work this week, so I'd guess the last four days (has it really only been four days?) is pretty typical of what Kathleen experiences all the time. The exception, of course, is that I have the hope of her coming back soon. So where I am only playing Mr. Mom for a few days, she has another 17 years or more.

I've been trying to do it all: quick runs to the grocery store, laundry, cleaning, schooling, comforting, etc... Several generous people have made us meals, so I'm not experiencing the full weight of mommy-hood, but I think I'm getting the picture. It's quite a job. At one point I was frantically running through the house trying to find my shoes so I could take Keziah (age 5) to the Emergency Room. All kinds of thoughts were running through my mind. "Should I leave the other kids alone while I go to the E.R?" "Can I call a neighbor?" "Do I have time to gel my hair?" (Hopefully I'm not that vain, but I had just gotten out of the shower.) It didn't even occur to me to call 911. I guess the little edible robots the kids made with toothpicks, marshmallows, and licorice weren't such a great idea. (To my credit, I didn't let them put toothpicks in the robots made for the smaller two kids.) Thankfully, she coughed up the toothpick before we made it out the door.

Another time I was pretty much at the end of my rope after Malia (age 3) missed the potty. I actually did okay with cleaning it up and all, but then later she was squirming around when I was putting her new pajamas on and I just about lost it. I didn't actually yell at her or do anything to her, but I admit, I most certainly felt like going berserk-o. What can I say? I've got testosterone issues. I'm just kidding, of course. The issues were not testosterone issues, but character issues. Actually, I was pretty discouraged by the whole event because I would like to think I'm a little more mature than that. God help me!

Then there was last night, or this morning, or whatever you want to call it. Jireh (18 months) woke up at 1:00

screaming. I dragged myself out of bed and got him some milk. That helped for a good five minutes and then he started at it again. I let him cry for another ten or fifteen minutes and then I went down to comfort him. Of course, two fears ruled my mind. First of all, what if he has an ear infection? Secondly, what if I can't get back to sleep? After thirty minutes or so of cuddling him and singing "Jesus Loves Me," I put him back down. Another thirty minutes or so and I was free to go back to sleep. That was several hours ago, and instead of lying in bed I'm writing all of you. (Maybe that's that whole thing about mommies wanting some adult companionship.) Anyway, of course the discouraging part of it all is that they're all going to start waking up in two hours. I've got a whole day ahead of me with very little rest. (That should really help my irritability issues, huh?)

The verse that comes to mind is Matthew 6:34. It says, "Therefore do not worry about tomorrow, for tomorrow will worry about itself. Each day has enough trouble of its own." I don't need to worry about tomorrow (or is it today now?). God will give me grace. He gave me grace to get through yesterday, and the day before, and the 14,000 and some days before that. There has never been a day that was too much. Sure, I might be a little sleepy, but maybe I'll get a nap, or Kath will come home early, or God will just help me minute by minute to keep faithfully serving Him right in the midst of my exhaustion. That's my hope. Somehow, someway, God is going to get me through today, and tomorrow, and the next 14,000 days after that. God is good.

A Perspective of Thankfulness

A Mike Lester cartoon pictured a housewife who was speaking to her husband who had evidently just returned home from the office. She said, "The water heater burst, the basement's flooded, the dishwasher overflowed, the dog has been "going" everywhere, the kids are tracking mud all over the house and yet...I feel like the luckiest woman on earth." She was holding a mop and on the table next to her was a newspaper with the headlines 'EARTHQUAKE TRIGGERS MASSIVE TSUNAMI KILLING THOUSANDS'.

This mommy's one-of-those-days was grabbed by the reality that even on one-of-those-days we don't necessarily have it all that bad. God has been kind to us – to all of us – in more ways than we can count.

I prefer modern music, but this reminds me of the old hymn that says, "Count your many blessings; name them one by one; count your blessings; see what God has done." Each of us would have a different list, but God has blessed us all: some with children, some with spouses, some with riches, some with health, some with friends, some with good looks, some with wisdom, and some with talents. None of us has been blessed in every realm, or maybe as much as we would desire, but we are still blessed. At a bare minimum we have

> Parenting can be hard. We all know that. But God wants us to maintain a spirit of thankfulness, not of resentment or regret.

been blessed with the gift of eternal life which is available for the taking by merely believing in Jesus. Even if that was all we had, that alone would be worth more than all the riches in the world!

Parenting can be hard. We all know that. But God wants us to maintain a spirit of thankfulness, not of resentment or regret. Enjoy your children and the difficulties that come with them. What fool after winning the lottery would resent all the shopping he has to do? God has blessed you immensely! Be thankful for how good you have it and remember all that God has done for you.

> *What fool after winning the lottery would resent all the shopping he has to do?*

Psalms 127:3 Sons are a heritage from the LORD, children a reward from Him.

1 Thessalonians 5:18 Give thanks in all circumstances, for this is God's will for you in Christ Jesus.

Give Them Something to Live For

In the teen years many Christian kids turn from the ways of their parents because they simply don't want to be like their parents. They have not seen a version of Christianity that is attractive and inspiring.

Kids today face a barrage of media influence. Millions are spent to capture your kids' hearts. Commercials constantly present their products as exciting and fulfilling. Drive our SUV and you can experience life on the edge! Movies present life as romance interspersed with thrilling car chases. Sports capture a desire we have to conquer and achieve. The message is loud and clear: if you want it all, it's yours for the taking. This can all have a pull on teens' hearts as they consider what kind of lifestyle they want to pursue.

Of course, there is the other option. You could get married and be true to just one person and have 1.8 children, a dog, and a white picket fence. You can work 50-60 hours a week, and maybe you'll earn enough to pay the bills. You can honor God by dressing out of style. Every Sunday you could go to church—twice. Don't forget Wednesday night prayer meetings! Each morning you could pray and read the Bible for 30 minutes. The message is loud and clear to many teens: run!

This is one of the problems with Christian families today. The kids don't want what we have. They don't want our families, lifestyles, churches, or our God.

I'm not saying we should throw all our energy into trying to compete with the media. I don't think we can win that battle with that approach. But we do need to give our kids something to live for. Even before their teen years kids need to understand that life is full of purpose.

One of the greatest purposes to live for is called the Great Commission. It was a call to action that Jesus gave to His followers repeatedly while here on the earth for 40 days after His resurrection. Given this context, it was obviously crucially important to Christ.

Matthew 28:18-20 Then Jesus came to them and said, "All authority in heaven and on earth has been given to me. Therefore go and make disciples of all nations, baptizing them in the name of the Father and of the Son and of the Holy Spirit, and teaching them to obey everything I have commanded you. And surely I am with you always, to the very end of the age."

This call to preach the good news is undoubtedly one of the greatest calls on a Christian's life. While it strikes fear into most of us, it also accomplishes something very important. It gives us purpose. It gives us something worth living for and something worth dying for.

Consider how this mission is being lived out in your home and in your family. Give attention to growth in this area. By the time your kids are teens they need to see this as a significant force in what drives your family to do the things you do. Your kids need to see very clearly that your life is being lived with intention.

We'll look at some specific ideas later on, but for now you may want to start brainstorming a few ideas of how you can take some steps in this area in your own life.

Being a United Force

Mark 3:25 [Jesus said,] "If a house is divided against itself, that house cannot stand."

It is hard to sufficiently underscore the importance of a husband and wife being united in their parenting.

Have you ever noticed how they put tar in the cracks on the highways? It costs a lot of money to go around filling millions of cracks. Why do they spend valuable resources that way? They do it because they know if they don't fix them, the cracks will spread and destroy the road. A little water gets into them, freezes and thaws a few times, and the crack widens and spreads. That is the way division works on roads. That's also how it works in churches, relationships, and marriages. A little division destroys everything.

Jesus said that a house divided "cannot stand!" Do not think that your house is the exception to this rule. Disunity will destroy your marriage and your family.

Since this is not a marriage book, I don't want to delve into this further. However, let me stress that if you and your spouse are disunited in your parenting, or in any area, this will have serious consequences on your children. It is difficult for healthy spiritual kids to come out of a divided home. You need to be humble and proactive here. Too much is at stake. Your marriage needs immediate attention. For starters, talk to your pastor and see if he can recommend someone who you can talk to. If you won't take this important step for yourselves, do it for your kids.

– 4 –

Parenting in Love

"And so we know and rely on the love God has for us. God is love. Whoever lives in love lives in God, and God in him."
—1 John 4:16

FROM OUR HOME

The Hearts of the Fathers

Malachi 4:6 "He will turn the hearts of the fathers to their children, and the hearts of the children to their fathers; or else I will come and strike the land with a curse."

To some fathers it may seem strange that a father's heart would have to be turned to his children. Some fathers seem to naturally enjoy a healthy relationship with their kids throughout the years.

However, it is much more difficult for other fathers. They may have once dreamed of playing catch with their kid some day, or of reading *The Hobbit* together on the couch, but it never quite worked out like that. They brought babies home from the hospital that were interested in nursing, not football. In fact, the whole first year of life seemed to be mommy's special time of bonding. Certainly things would get better with age...wouldn't they?

As their babies grew, bonding with their children did not become any more natural. When their babies cried, they wanted their mommies. When they got hurt, they wanted their mommies. When they needed comfort, they wanted their mommies. In fact, they always wanted their mommies.

Some of these dads gave up. They felt out of place, unneeded, and even a little rejected. They felt that since mommy seemed so gifted at parenting, they should just step back and get out of the way. They gave themselves to their careers, their hobbies, and even their churches, but they never learned how to connect with their kids. The time for reading to their kids came and went, and passing the football together never quite interested them or their children.

If you're one of those dads, something needs to change. Your heart needs to be turned back to your kid, and your kid's heart needs to be turned back to you. It may seem awkward for you, but you've got to connect with your kid no matter what it takes.

Let me give you the secret for connecting with your preteen child. It's wrestling. You don't need to know how. You're bigger. You'll figure it out. Get down on the floor, and in a taunting tone, say something like, "Come 'ere boy. Let me show you the double leg grab pull down flip around." If he squeals with laughter, take him down. If he runs, hunt him down.

I don't mean to imply that wrestling is all that there is to connecting with younger kids. That would be absurd. There is also tickling. Tickle a lot. Tickle their feet, their arms, their legs, their necks. Some people think that too much tickling is cruel, and those people should be thankful that I was not their father, because I would have tickled such silly notions right out of them.

Of course these two keys to parenting can also be combined. Unlike collegiate wrestling, tickling is the ultimate goal of the match. You don't take them down so that you can count to three; you take them down so that you can tickle them.

I hope you know I'm not kidding. It obviously doesn't have to be wrestling and tickling but you've got to connect with your kid. Get down on the ground and spend an hour with your child. Get at his level and wrestle or play Legos®. Build a model, have a pillow fight, or play Hot Wheels®. Try to be a kid for a little while.

You don't have to be Super Dad. You don't have to be too creative. They just want you. They want your time and your attention. Give them your heart, and they'll give you theirs in return.

Strong Moms and Involved Dads

There are two common fatal blunders that many parents make. One is that they are too soft on their kids and don't correct, train, or discipline them enough. The other is that they don't express enough love to their kids. Many people seem to think they need to stress one or the other, as if love and discipline were two opposites. *That is wrong thinking.* Love and discipline go hand-in-hand. The Bible says that "If you love your children, you will correct them."[22] A balanced parent is one who shows love through affection and discipline. Most parents need to greatly increase their efforts in one of these areas. They may think they are being loving by being overly permissive, or they may be strict without expressing love, but they need to be strong in both love and discipline.

Oftentimes each parent is weak in one of these two areas. The typical pattern is that the mom is not as strong as she needs to be and that the dad is not as involved or loving as he needs to be. If you've ever watched Nanny 911 or Super Nanny, you've seen this played out in almost every episode. While you might think this is the perfect balance, the reality is that

[22] Proverbs 13:24 (NCV)

your kids will someday evaluate you on an individual basis. They'll say things like, "Dad was never around," or "Dad never once said, 'I love you.'" They aren't likely to say, "Dad was never around, but Mom made up for it by always being there for me." Kids don't get enough love from mom; they need it from dad too. The same goes for discipline.

We'll deal with discipline in much more depth later on, but what do you think happens when a parent is strict without also being expressively loving? You guessed it. The kids pull away. As a friend of mine says, "Rules without relationship results in rebellion." If a child doesn't sense a strong message of love from you, then he will naturally pull away from you when you give him instruction or correction.

A healthy spiritual home desperately needs the balanced presence of both love and discipline. Does your home have a balanced presence of both love and discipline?

Balance Correction and Positive Input

1 Peter 4:8 Above all, love each other deeply, because love covers over a multitude of sins.

I was once taught that you should praise someone more than you correct him. I don't know whether or not that is the perfect balance, but it is valuable to know that there is a need for balance and to figure out what that looks like for your own family.

I remember a regional manager I had in high school when I worked as a cook in a restaurant. He was a perfectionist to the extreme. Nothing was ever done to his satisfaction. He corrected everything I did. Nothing was ever done fast enough or well enough. Even when I would stay late to help he'd be upset that I was costing the company overtime. There was just no way to win. He drove me crazy. But every time I finished a shift, he would call to me from the office as I was leaving, "Steve, come here." I'd poke my head into his office and he'd always give me a verbal pat on the back by looking me in the eye and saying something like, "You did a good job today." It's likely the only thing that kept me from quitting. His "love" expressed at the end of the day covered over a multitude of his "sins."

In parenting, kids need constant correction. That means they need constant affirmation as well. A hug, a smile, a wink, a tease, a tickle and a frequent "I love you" go a long way. If they feel we are constantly riding them, they will become discouraged. If we are constantly reaffirming them and not correcting them, they will become self-centered. A good healthy dose of correction and affirmation will do wonders for them.

Colossians 3:21 Fathers, do not embitter your children, or they will become discouraged.

I Love You

Too many parents think that it is enough to simply provide for their kids and to make sure they get their basic needs met. While that is certainly important, kids want to hear the words, "I love you." That is awkward for some people (especially males). Maybe you weren't raised that way, or no one in your family said, "I love you." Perhaps you think that not showing love is simply a family thing—part of your heritage.

The catch is that you are not just a Nelson (or whoever you are). You are not just Dutch (or whatever you are). You are a Christian. As Christians we are not called to act according to our upbringing. We are called to act according to the will of God.

Look at these two separate instances recorded in the Bible.

The first was at Jesus' baptism; the second was at His transfiguration.

Matthew 3:17 And a voice from heaven said, "This is my Son, <u>whom I love</u>; with Him I am well pleased."

Matthew 17:5 While [Peter] was still speaking, a bright cloud enveloped them, and a voice from the cloud said, "This is my Son, <u>whom I love</u>; with Him I am well pleased. Listen to Him!"

God the Father audibly communicated His love for Jesus on two occasions. In fact, these occasions are two of only three direct communications from the Father to the Son during His 33 years on the earth. God must have thought that was a pretty important thing to communicate, don't you think? God even did this in the hearing of Jesus' followers. He was not embarrassed to tell others of His love. Are you embarrassed to tell your children you love them? If so, why?

I have no idea what your upbringing was, but do you wish your parents would have said, "I love you" more, or less? Some of us had parents that said it frequently, and some never said it at all, but can you imagine *anyone* wanting to hear it less? That is hard for me to imagine. Words of affirmation mean the world to us, and that is especially true when those words are from our parents.

The verse commonly called the Golden Rule says, "So in everything, do to others what you would have them do to you," (Matthew 7:12a). Another way of wording it would be to treat others as you would want to be treated. If you would have wanted your parents to say "I love you" a little more, then don't you think *your* kids would want the same? Isn't that doing to others what you would have them do to you?

This comes so unnaturally to some that they think that

saying it once a year is being overly affectionate. Is it? Is that all that you would have wanted from your parents? You may want to try saying it daily—every night before bed, or every morning when you first see your child. "Good morning, Keziah. It's good to see you this morning. Do you know that I love you? You're sure special to me." Wouldn't you like that kind of treatment every morning, or even throughout the day? It's not that life has to be a continual hug fest, but we do try to constantly communicate love.

Both Kathleen and I tell each of our kids we love them every single day. In fact, it is far more frequent than that. We say, "I love you," with our actions as well, but we are careful not to neglect saying it with our words. Vary rarely do we have *any* interaction with our kids where we do not express our love to them in some fashion.

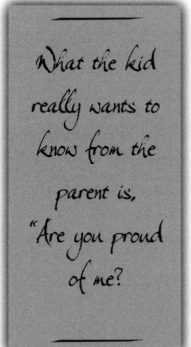

What the kid really wants to know from the parent is, "Are you proud of me?"

I'm Proud of You

Most kids know that their parents love them, but that is sometimes a hollow victory for the parent. Saying the words meets a need, but it is only the most basic of needs. What the kid really wants to know from the parent is, "Are you proud of me? Are you pleased with me?"

In counseling, I've asked a number of teenagers if they felt that their parents loved them. Most say that they do. When I ask if they feel that their parents are proud of them, most say "No," and that is what really matters to the kid.

Why is that what matters? Because the teens often feel that love is obligatory. It's like we *have* to love them because they are our children. We *have* to love them because God says we should. We *have* to love them because love is supposed to be unconditional. What they really want to know is that we are pleased with them.

Let's take another look at what God the Father said to Jesus:

Matthew 3:17 And a voice from heaven said, "This is my Son, whom I love; with Him I am well pleased."

Matthew 17:5 While [Peter] was still speaking, a bright cloud enveloped them, and a voice from the cloud said, "This is my Son, whom I love; with Him I am well pleased. Listen to Him!"

God communicated His love for Christ and His pleasure. This can be a difficult thing when a kid is acting up, which of course, is typically the case when I'm counseling them. So how can a parent communicate pleasure when a child is not being particularly pleasing?

It is helpful to look at it as we view our relationship with God. Do you know that God loves you? Of course.[23] Do you know that God is pleased with you? You should.[24] Unless you are in outright rebellion and sin, you should know that God is pleased with you. How can we know that God is pleased with us when we are constantly sinning? We know that God has forgiven our sins, but we also know that God shows grace. God knows we are not perfect. He knows that we are going to continue to fail, but He is pleased with our faith[25] as we stumble

---

[23] John 3:16; Romans 5:8; 8:31-39; Ephesians 2:4; 3:17-19; 1 John 3:1,16
[24] Colossians 1:10; 1 Thessalonians 4:1; Hebrews 11:5,6; Hebrews 13:16
[25] Romans 14:23; Galatians 5:6; Ephesians 3:12; Hebrews 11:5,6

along through life trying to follow Him.

Is it possible to displease God? Although every sin is in some way displeasing, God's displeasure should not typically define our relationship. Generally, God is pleased with us. However, if you turn from Him and are unwilling to change, does that displease God? I believe it does. He was certainly displeased with Ananias,[26] Simon,[27] and with the people listed as examples for us in 1 Corinthians 10.[28] Grievous sin grieves God. Let there be no doubt about that. However, even when God is displeased, His pleasure is not hard to get back. God is a compassionate Father.

> *Psalms 103:8-14 The LORD is compassionate and gracious, slow to anger, abounding in love. He will not always accuse, nor will He harbor His anger forever; He does not treat us as our sins deserve or repay us according to our iniquities. For as high as the heavens are above the earth, so great is His love for those who fear Him; as far as the east is from the west, so far has He removed our transgressions from us. As a father has compassion on his children, so the LORD has compassion on those who fear Him; for He knows how we are formed, He remembers that we are dust.*

In the story of the prodigal son,[29] do you think that the father was pleased with his son when he was off squandering his inheritance on wild living? I'm sure he wasn't terribly pleased, even though he still loved the son deeply and longed for his return. Yet when the son returned, the father gave his immediate and wholehearted blessing. He was so excited that he threw him a party! This was not just an obligatory love. He

[26] Acts 5:1-10,
[27] Acts 8:18-24
[28] 1 Corinthians 10:1-11
[29] Luke 15:11-32

wanted to show off his son and celebrate. The father's actions communicated the message that he was extremely proud that the boy was his son, and he was exceptionally glad to have him back. His response communicated pride and pleasure, not just love.

With our own children, we need to be careful not to be stingy in showing pleasure. Our children should feel our pleasure the vast majority of the time. In the rare event that our children rebel to the point of losing our pleasure, it needs to be readily available again the moment our children turn back to us.

Psalms 30:5a For His anger lasts only a moment, but His favor lasts a lifetime.

Do we ever get upset at our kids? Sure. Do we ever get disappointed? Yes. But, like God, our anger should only be momentary, while our favor needs to be lifelong. We'll even say these words to our kids to let them know that we are for them. "Honey, I might be upset with you for this moment, but how long does my favor last?" They smile and say, "For a lifetime."

Like God, our anger should only be momentary, while our favor needs to be lifelong.

Did you know that a church can hire consultants to come in and evaluate everything they do? Imagine having a consultant spend two weeks learning about your church and what it believes and does, observing every meeting and event. Now, can you imagine the consultant giving the church a copy of his report, which outlines multiple glaring faults in the church, and concluding by saying that your church meetings do more harm than good?

1 Corinthians 11:17 In the following directives I have no praise for you, for your meetings do more harm than good.

Those are harsh words from Paul to the church in Corinth. They must have had numerous serious issues to earn such a rebuke. By the time Paul wrote his second letter to the church in Corinth, some of their problems had been dealt with. However, they still had issues, and were by no means a perfect church made up of perfect people. Yet look at what Paul wrote in his second letter:

2 Corinthians 7:4 I have great confidence in you; I take great pride in you. I am greatly encouraged; in all our troubles my joy knows no bounds.

Can you imagine saying this to your child after he comes back to you after a period of sin and rebellion? "I am confident in you. I am proud of you. I couldn't be any happier." It is true that a wayward child needs to repent, but when he does, a parent must be quick to show grace and forgiveness, just as our Lord does to us.

We are fragile people. We can easily be crushed if we feel a lack of approval from our parents. Do your kids a favor and regularly communicate your pleasure through both your words and your actions!

This Is My Child

For many people, love can be performance-based. I know a number of people who, even in their adulthood, would give anything to 'earn' their parents' approval. With some parents it is subtle; with others it is obvious. They place their own value as a person in their children, and then they seek the praise of others through their child's academics, attractiveness, athletics, or abilities. Sometimes it is almost as if they were trying to live through their children.

Our children need to see that they have value apart from their achievements. Let's take one more look at what God the Father said about Jesus:

Matthew 3:17 And a voice from heaven said, "This is my Son, whom I love; with Him I am well pleased."

Matthew 17:5 While [Peter] was still speaking, a bright cloud enveloped them, and a voice from the cloud said, "This is my Son, whom I love; with Him I am well pleased. Listen to Him!"

Saying "This is my Son," communicates belonging. It says, "You are mine and I love you, not because of what you do, but because you are mine." Our children need to hear that from us. They are special, not because of what they do, but because they are ours.

There are lots of kids whom I love and care about, but none of them are like my own. It's not because mine are better but simply because they are mine. God made it that way. I'll ask my kids if they know why I love them, and then I'll tell them that I love them because they are mine. There is security in that. No matter what they do, they will always be mine, and I will always love them just for that.

We will often tell the kids things like, "We are so thankful that God gave you to us to raise. We are so grateful that we get to be your parents." This is not to inflate their egos, but to help them understand that they belong. They are ours!

God-time, God-talk, and God-giving

1 John 3:18 Dear children, let us not love with words or tongue but with actions and in truth.

I know that you love your kids. If you didn't love your kids, you wouldn't care enough to be reading this book. The question is not just whether or not you love your kids, but do your kids *feel* loved? Have you expressed your love to your kids adequately?

The simplest way to communicate love is to say the three magic words: "I love you." But there are many ways to communicate love. There are hugs, pats on the head, kind words, words of praise, winks, goodnight kisses, and the list goes on.

I once heard that there are three ways to tell where a person's priorities are. You can tell by where they spend their time, what they think about, and on what they spend their money. You may want to think about this in relationship to your children. If you tell them you love them but you are always working on your classic car, always talking about cars, and spending all the family's money on cars, what message do you think they are going to get? If they are minimally bright they'll figure out that what you really love is your car.

Our first priority revealer is time. You need to spend time with your kids. There is no greater sacrifice than to play Candy Land®[30] with your child. If that is not dying to yourself, I don't

[30] Candy Land is a registered trademark of Hasbro.

know what is. You don't always have to play games, Barbies®, and Super Nintendo®, but you need to spend some time. If you really want to spend some quality time together, try to spend some God-time together.

A couple of years ago we started a simple time of Bible reading and prayer every morning at our house with some of the church guys that lived nearby. Pretty soon my son wanted to join. Within a year my daughter wanted to join, followed shortly by my second son. Now everyone in my family who can read starts almost every day together for 40 minutes of God-time, while the little ones snuggle or play quietly on a blanket. We've had a fantastic time discovering God together.

I was out praying on our balcony one night, and my eight-year-old, Silas, came out and prayed with me for a few minutes. A few days later Kathleen asked him, "What is your favorite thing to do with Daddy?" He smiled and said, "I know! Pray with him."

God-time spent with your children is time well spent and much less painful than Candy Land®.

Examining our thoughts is the next way to tell where our priorities lie. Most of us would rate God and family as two of our top priorities. Is that reflected in our thoughts? How can you tell? Jesus said, "Out of the overflow of the heart the mouth speaks" (Matthew 12:34). What you talk about is a window to what is going on in your heart. Your conversation should be filled with God-talk and family talk. If your conversations always revolve around sports, hobbies, shopping, or crafts, then your kids will easily feel like they are playing second fiddle.

Stop for a minute. What do you honestly spend the majority of your time thinking about? Do you think about things related to God or your family? If most of our thoughts are not consumed by these top priorities, then we've got to stop and question what is really important to us.

Our final priority revealer is money. Money is given to

us primarily to bless other people. Jesus said, *"Do not store up for yourselves treasures on earth, where moth and rust destroy, and where thieves break in and steal. But store up for yourselves treasures in heaven, where moth and rust do not destroy, and where thieves do not break in and steal"* (Matthew 6:19-20). So, how do we store up treasures in heaven? We store up treasures in heaven by not storing them up here. Our treasures here are given to us so that we can bless others. We bless our spouses, our kids, and our churches. We should also bless the poor, the needy, and the destitute. If we tell our kids we love them but we spend our money extravagantly and wastefully instead of putting food on the table, then they are going to have a hard time believing we love them. By the same token, if we tell them that we love God, and that they should love God, but then we don't give to God, they will eventually detect our hypocrisy.

Words are powerful, but at times actions speak louder than words. We need to love with our actions, as well as with our words.

FROM OUR HOME

Baseballs and Bike Chains

"And if anyone gives even a cup of cold water to one of these little ones because he is my disciple, I tell you the truth, he will certainly not lose his reward." Matthew 10:42

"Daddy, how come you have time to go to a baseball game tonight, but you don't have time to fix my bike chain?" asked my 6-year-old.

"Well, buddy," I started to explain, "it's not quite that simple." "You see it's part of my job to go to the game since it's a church activity." Of course, I immediately realized that sounded pretty stupid, so I set to work on fixing his chain as I continued defending my actions. I mumbled on for a few minutes vainly trying to make my priorities sound reasonable, but, of course, that was a lost cause. Fortunately, six-year-olds are more interested in getting their bikes fixed than on scrutinizing faulty logic.

It's funny that I thought I could watch baseball for Jesus, but I didn't have time to help my own son for five minutes for Jesus. It sure seemed pretty obvious to my son what the right thing to do was, but somehow I missed it. Sometimes I get fooled into thinking that simple acts of kindness are unspiritual work. Going to church, serving in ministries, and reading my Bible all seem to be spiritual work (and let's not forget attending baseball games), but somehow fixing a bike chain seems different.

I wonder how often we miss opportunities to serve Jesus because we don't view ordinary acts of kindness as being spiritual. Does giving someone a cup of cold water only count if they are dressed in rags, or does it also count if they are 3 ½ feet tall and their cup has a spill-proof lid on it? We need to remind ourselves that even the most ordinary acts of kindness are spiritual works that please God—even putting on bike chains.

They Want You!

It shouldn't be a surprise to anyone that one of the greatest competitors of the family is the workplace. Let's face it—if you don't put in your time, you get fired. Actually, more and more it seems like you have to put in your time and then some. Some of this is unavoidable. You do have to put food on the table, and you do have to have a roof over your head. However, because your job comes with built-in and immediate consequences for not performing well, it is easy to prioritize work over family. After all, when was the last time you got a yearly review as a parent? When have you ever feared being replaced as a parent, or felt that if you didn't put in your time someone would ask you to start looking for a new family?

If surveyed, I think the vast majority of us would say that we prioritize family time over work, but since work is evaluated, it is easy to live contrary to our stated priorities. We can always catch up on family time on the weekend, or maybe next weekend, or perhaps on the next holiday, or maybe in six months when things are really supposed to slow down at work… But product needs to go out the door now, and projects need to be completed yesterday, if not sooner.

One common deception is to think that you are critically important at work, but at home you're somewhat expendable. Your spouse, or even someone else, can pick up the slack at home, but no one can pick up the slack at work. Or can they? The very fact that you can be fired implies that someone else can do your job, or that your job can even go undone. The fact that you can't be fired at home highlights your need to be there. No one else will do your job.

Just before becoming a pastor I was an Oracle developer (computer programmer) for Woodward Governor Company. When I left the company I left several folders full of notes and I told my boss, "If you ever need me to come back and troubleshoot some of these programs, I'll need these notes to refresh my memory." I knew I wasn't indispensable, but, well, you just hope that no one else can quite fill your shoes. Interestingly enough, I never got a call for any emergency consulting. The computer programs didn't crash. Productivity didn't come to a screeching halt in my absence. In fact, ten years later, the company is doing just fine without me.

My kids, however, need *me*. If I don't spend fatherly time with them, no one else will. Babysitters can watch them, and teachers can educate them, but no one else will be their dad. They don't just need someone to do the tasks of parenting; they need someone to be their parent. In counseling sessions no one has ever said to me, "My dad was never home, but, on the bright side, I really liked my babysitter." When it comes to evaluating their disappointments in life, kids don't measure the quality of their care. They measure the quality and quantity of time that their parents spend with them.

Obviously we're all going to have people watch our kids at times for different reasons, and someone needs to bring home the bacon. Both parents can't be home with their kids 24-7. I'm not saying that. I'm just saying that we need to be careful not to fall into the trap of thinking that we are indispensable at work, but that at home everyone can get along without us just fine.

Here are some questions that you may want to use to evaluate your own situation:

+ Am I willing to cut back on extra work time even if it means my reviews may take a hit?

+ Will I turn down a promotion if it negatively impacts my family?

+ We all need to go the extra mile at times, but for how many weeks or months will I allow my job to come before my family time?

+ Am I willing to severely adjust my mortgage payment, car payment, and lifestyle to accommodate a change to a lower paying and more family-friendly job?

None of these questions are easy, and there are no pat answers. However, in setting or resetting our priorities, it would be good to at least consider: at what cost do we succeed at work? If you think you may be out of balance in this, or in any area of parenting, by all means, talk to a trusted Christian friend about it and get an outside opinion.

At what cost do we succeed at work?

Proverbs 15:22 Plans fail for lack of counsel, but with many advisers they succeed.

Eye Twinkles

In an effort to pray more, I recently went out for a prayer walk around the park. I was running out of things to pray for, so I just started thanking God for everything I saw that I liked. "Thanks, God, for the lake. Thanks for how the water ripples and for its soothing sounds. Thanks for crickets chirping. Thanks for pinecones. They look so fascinating and they are fun to throw. Thanks for maple trees and those little whirlybird seeds they have. How cool is that?..."

At first this seemed to me to be a childish exercise, but after about five minutes I was really getting into it. The more things I thought of, the more appreciative I became, and the more excited about God I got. Pretty soon I had a smile on my face and a twinkle in my eye. I was so touched by my Father and His love for me.

If you stop and think about it a minute, you will realize that your heavenly Father has captured your heart by what He has done for you. Is there anything that you can do for your children that can capture their hearts? What would make their eyes twinkle? Maybe it is coming home from work early one day, or meeting them at school for lunch. Perhaps it is yelling, "I'm proud of you," at their game in front of their friends. Could you "camp out" with them in the living room, or get up and watch the sunrise? Have you ever tried having communion together as a family, or singing worship songs around a campfire? Maybe you could even sing a wild song with them as you dance around the living room.

I read a story to the kids called "Tenderly Forever."[31] It's about a dad who wrote letters to his daughter every year on her birthday and sealed them and kept them in a box. When she turned seventeen he put them all in a leather binding and gave them to her all at once. How powerful would that be?

Kathleen will often catch Keziah (or any of our children) and say something like, "If God lined up all the little six-year-olds in the world and said I could just pick one, do you know who I'd pick?"

Keziah's eyes will sparkle and she'll giggle and say, "Who?"

"I'd work my way all the way down to the end of the line until I found a little dirty-faced, curly-haired girl named Keziah, and I'd pick you."

As there are limitless ways that God has shown His love, there are limitless ways to touch your children. What can you do to make their eyes light up today?

The Joy of Parenting

I remember when, a year ago or so, we had 'one of those nights.' One of the girls was sick and getting up every ten or fifteen minutes to go to the bathroom. After each trip to the bathroom she'd come back and roll on our floor moaning with

---

[31] Author unknown. From *Heart to Heart Stories for Dads*, compiled and edited by Joe Wheeler.

a cramping stomach. (Our bedroom floor is the makeshift infirmary as well as refuge from all things that are scary.) We were both drifting in and out of sleep until around midnight when Kathleen got concerned and called the doctor. After being sick all day, we were concerned that our girl might be getting dehydrated. The doctor reassured us that there wasn't much that could be done, so Kathleen tried to treat some of the symptoms. She put a heating pad on her stomach and gave her some pain killer as well. Do you remember what happened when you were a kid and your mom gave you medicine? Yeah. That happened. She threw it up along with what seemed to be several meals all over the bathroom floor. Unfortunately Kathleen was in the way and got her feet nailed as well. I scrambled out of bed and started helping the cleanup process. I think we were back in bed around 2:00.

Actually, we've had some worse incidents where several kids were getting sick all at once. I remember that one of those nights was the night before going in for a scheduled c-section. After the entire night of cleaning up after sick children, we finally just gave up trying to sleep and just sat in bed and talked while we waited for morning to come.

Sometimes it's not illness, but nightmares. There's nothing like getting awakened by a blood-curdling scream and then trying to comfort a child who isn't quite back into our space-time continuum yet.

And then there's the nightly stuff: nursing, children falling out of bed, bathroom runs, dropped stuffed animals, and complaints of "I can't sleep," "I'm thirsty," and "I'm scared." We've even had them wake us up ("us" meaning "Kathleen") just to say, "I love you."

Of course parenting is exhausting much of the time, but I mention nighttime because that can be when all our frustrations come to a culmination. It's hard enough to survive the demands of the day, but can't we at least get a reprieve? Is a night's sleep too much to ask? Nighttime is also when we are really not in the mood to die to ourselves and serve others. We want to sleep, not clean up vomit.

Oftentimes, parenting leaves no choice. When a child throws up, you have to clean it up whether you feel like it or not. (As if you'd ever feel like it, right?) It's not like a job where you can just leave and find a different place of employment. You can't get a transfer to an easier position. You just do what needs to be done, when it needs to be done. There is often little choice in that.

However, there is choice in this: you can choose how you respond. You can respond in anger, or with a grumbling heart, or you can respond cheerfully, out of a good heart.

In 1 Peter 5:2 pastors are called to be "eager to serve." It is not enough that we serve, that we do the job and complete the task, but we are to have a heart and passion for it. We should be "eager" to do it. Isn't that true of all service? Who wants a grumbling employee, child, or even waitress? We'd much rather have service with a smile.

Certainly God wants us to serve Him through serving the children He has given us, but He also wants us to do it with a good heart—to embrace our cross, so to speak. Although serving God is good, serving with a good heart is vastly superior. He asks us to be cheerful givers (2 Corinthians 9:7) and cheerful mercy givers (Romans 12:8). He tells us not to complain (Philippians 2:14), to offer hospitality without grumbling (1 Peter 4:9), and to serve wholeheartedly (Ephesians 6:7). Certainly, if He wants this kind of cheerful service in the Christian life, He also wants this kind of service in the Christian home. That's not too much of a stretch, is it?

Perhaps the key is remembering that it is Christ we are serving. After all, if He were staying at my house, I wouldn't get mad if He woke me up; and if He got sick, I'd be honored to clean up after Him. It would be a privilege. So if the child God entrusted to my care needs the same level of sacrifice from me, should I respond any differently? Shouldn't it still be an honor to serve God's child?

Don't let parenting be a burdensome drudgery. Find joy in your parenting. Be eager to serve, and choose to respond according to God's power and not your own "sleepy" flesh.

Matthew 10:42 [Jesus said,] "And if anyone gives even a cup of cold water to one of these little ones because he is my disciple, I tell you the truth, he will certainly not lose his reward."

Quality Time

"Hey, honey. I'm going to have a really busy week. On Thursday night I should have about thirty minutes that we can spend together, but we'll make it a really quality time. Sorry, but that's all I have." That doesn't work in a marriage, does it? It doesn't work in parenting either.

One night, I was driving with a couple of the kids, which is all we had at the time. We were singing a little song I made up about the Golden Rule, which is hard to describe in words, but it is pretty cool if I may say so myself. Then we started singing "Love the Lord your God" to the tune of the Beatles' "All You Need Is Love." We were all going crazy singing at the top of our voices and then I noticed the Hale-Bopp comet. I pointed it out to the kids and we talked about that for a while, and about how awesome God is for creating the heavens and cool stuff like that. It was a really sweet time.

Don't think that I am always that creative and think of just the right things to do, say, and sing. We'd had many, many uneventful drives before that night, and have had many since that night, but that one drive was special. Why? I don't know. It just happened.

You can't easily plan quality time; it just happens—and it happens with quantity time. The more time you spend to-gether, the more likely that some of that time will be special. The same is true of your time with your spouse, with God, or with anyone else.

I think about John leaning back on Jesus at the Last Supper.[32] I'm not sure if that was necessarily on Jesus' agenda for the evening, but it happened amidst time that they spent together. I wonder if specific quality events like that are what made John refer to himself as the disciple whom Jesus loved.[33] But they weren't just little snippets of time here and there. John spent day in and day out with Jesus—walking, talking, and serving together. They lived their lives together.

Quality time comes with quantity time.

If you want quality moments with your kids, make it a pri-ority to spend time with your family. *Make no mistake about it, quality time comes with quantity time.*

---

[32] John 21:20
[33] John 13:23; 20:2; 21:7; 21:20

– 5 –

Discipline

"The parent must convince himself that discipline is not something he does to the child; it is something he does for the child."
—James C. Dobson

Discipline Introduction

Whenever I pick up a book on parenting I always go straight to the chapter on discipline. For me, it is a watershed issue on whether or not a book is worth its weight in pulp. Some of you reading this now may be doing the same. Since we share this quirk, it is hard for me to complain about you skipping over much of the material that helps provide some balance, but let me say just one thing: parenting is not all about discipline. Discipline can help restore order and peace to your home, but it is not a cure-all. Parenting is more complicated than that. Discipline is important in parenting, but so are love, training, vision, involvement, your example, and a number of other things.

In basketball, making a basket may seem like the most important part of the game, but jumping, dribbling, defense, and passing are equally important. It's the same thing with parenting and discipline. If you want to win with your kids, it is not enough to focus on discipline.

That said, biblical discipline can make a colossal difference in your home. Please try to set aside your established ideas about discipline and take a moment to study the timeless truths of God's Word in this area. People have many fears and preconceived ideas about what constitutes loving and appropriate discipline.

> Discipline is important in parenting, but so are love, training, vision, involvement, your example, and a number of other things.

As you read, try not to jump to conclusions or pass judgment. Read through to the end and give thought to the Scriptures written here. Ask God to give you discernment.

Bonsai Parenting

Do you know what a bonsai tree is? For those of you who don't, a bonsai tree is a miniaturized adult tree. It's not a specific type of tree. It can be a pine, oak, maple, or any number of types of trees, but it is just a fraction of the size of a normal tree. It is grown in a small pot or tray, and it is never allowed to grow any bigger than a foot or two tall. The gardener takes the plant and prunes it whenever it gets too big, and once a year the gardener will even uproot the tree and prune the roots. The result is that, after years and years, the gardener produces a tree that has the appearance of being full grown in that its bark looks aged and it has thick branches, but the tree is only a foot or two tall.

Why would a gardener do such a thing? He does it because he has a vision for how he wants the tree to look. He knows that the tree is not likely to just happen to grow into the specific design that he has pictured in his mind. Without trimming it, it will grow into a large, wild, unrestrained tree that you would never want in your house. With consistent pruning and restraint, the tree is allowed to develop its own shape and character, but within constraints and boundaries. It is restrained from becoming what it would be if left to its own, and it is shaped into a beautiful creation.

This is similar to how it works with children. If you restrain them, discipline them, and stop them from becoming what they would naturally turn into, you end up with a well-trained child, teenager, or young adult who is pleasant and a joy to have in your home. If you don't, you may end up with a kid who drives you crazy, robs you of peace, and, like Eli's sons, makes you wonder, "Why do you do such things?"[34]

While some trees grow beautifully without pruning, there are also some that don't. We have a magnificent white fir on our property that is about seventy feet tall. It is nothing less than majestic even though it has never been pruned. We also have some cedars and junipers that are huge overgrown eyesores. They are past the stage where pruning can accomplish much, and at this point they are just unsightly. Most of us would agree that unrestrained children are more likely to become uncontrolled junipers rather than magnificent white firs. A well-trained child is typically a result of years and years of intensive parenting, not a consequence of a hands-off approach.

Many parents today have been taught that they should not interfere too much with their children. They've been taught to let their children grow into whatever their natural bent is. Unfortunately, a child's natural bent is evil. I hope that doesn't surprise you. I assume you've seen some of the signs. Has your baby ever screamed in anger so loud that the veins were popping out of her neck? Has your two-year-old taken away a toy from another toddler and hit him over the head with it? Has your ten-year-old screamed, "I hate you"? Concerning your teenager, have you ever received a dreaded call from a teacher, the principal, or the police? If so, then this concept shouldn't be too shocking. A child's natural inclination is not toward good. It is toward evil. In other words, you have not had to train your child to act in rebellious and defiant ways. It all came quite naturally.

God put it this way:

---

[34] 1 Samuel 2:23

Genesis 6:5 The LORD saw how great man's wickedness on the earth had become, and that every inclination of the thoughts of his heart was only evil all the time.

Genesis 8:21 ...every inclination of [man's] heart is evil from childhood...

Psalms 51:5 Surely I was sinful at birth, sinful from the time my mother conceived me.

No one needs to train your child how to be a wild shoot. You need to train your child how not to be one. If you want your child to be selfish, rebellious, arrogant, violent, and lazy, you do not have to lift a finger. Just provide food and shelter and she will grow into those things. Without proper training, a parent's greatest fears are quite likely to be lived out: promiscuity, drugs, alcohol, dropping out, etc... It's all preprogrammed. If you have a different vision for your child, a godly vision, then you need to train your child by restraining her, disciplining her, and stopping her from growing into what comes naturally.

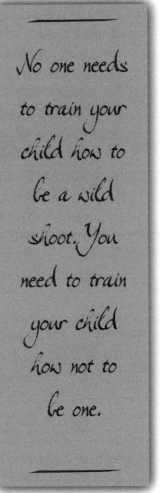

Many parents fail in this, but this is to what you and I are called. We are charged by God to shape our children into something beautiful, and this is one of our greatest tasks as parents.

Eli's Unrestrained Sons

Eli was a priest in the Old Testament right at the end of the days of the Judges and just before the period when the kings began to rule over Israel. Or if it is more helpful to think of it this way, he was right after Samson and right before Samuel, Saul, and David.

Eli had a problem. His sons were totally out of control. In 1 Samuel chapters 1 and 3 it says that they had no regard for the LORD, sinned against the LORD, did not listen to their father's rebuke, and made themselves contemptible. They were known for their wicked deeds, and their sin was great in the LORD's sight. Specifically, they were stealing sacrifices from the LORD (1 Samuel 2:12-17) and sleeping with the women who served at the entrance of the Tent of Meeting (1 Samuel 2:22). Simply put, Eli's sons were every parent's nightmare.

Because of these sins God said that both of Eli's sons would die on the same day and that the priesthood would be taken away from Eli's house (1 Samuel 2:30-36). True to the LORD's word, Eli's sons both died in battle on the same day (1 Samuel 4:11). When Eli heard that the ark of God had also been captured in that battle, he fell out of his chair, broke his neck, and died. After his death Samuel, who was essentially Eli's adopted son, became the new priest, and so the priesthood left Eli's family, just as God had determined.

So why was Eli held partially responsible for the sins of his sons? In 1 Samuel 3:13, God said the following about Eli, "For I told him that I would judge his family forever because of the sin he knew about; his sons made themselves contemptible, and he failed to restrain them." Eli failed at restraining his sons. Other translations phrase it by saying that he did not stop them, discipline them, or rebuke them. Parent, you must understand that it is your job to restrain your children, and that this is a job that God takes seriously. God dealt directly and severely with Eli for failing to redirect the course of his children's lives. Without a doubt, God held Eli responsible for not stepping in and not parenting his sons well. It would be wise for us to sit up and take note of this and learn from Eli's poor example.

It is also interesting to note the ages of Eli's sons. Their actions indicate that they were old enough to be sleeping with women (1 Samuel 2:22) and big and strong enough to physically threaten men (1 Samuel 2:16). Certainly they were in their late teens if not older than that. Yet God didn't let Eli off the hook just because his kids were old enough to give an account for their own actions. God did hold them accountable, but He also held their father accountable for his failure to step in and restrain them.

Disobedience and rebellion in our children is our problem.

Eli was not punished for the evil behavior of his kids. He was punished for failing to do anything about it. He could have removed them from the positions they were abusing, turned them over to the authorities, or punished them in some other manner. Had he done something, he would not have been punished for their actions.

I'm not saying that God is going to strike you dead for failing to discipline; I'm just saying that God wants parents to take responsibility for their kids. God saw the problem with Eli's sons, but He also saw Eli's problem. Before our children are full-grown and out of the house, we've got to view disobedience and rebellion in *our* children as *our* problem.

Interfere with Your Children

1 Kings 1:5,6 Now Adonijah, whose mother was Haggith, put himself forward and said, "I will be king." So he got chariots and horses ready, with fifty men to run ahead of him. (His father had never interfered with him by asking, "Why do you behave as you do?" He was also very handsome and was born next after Absalom.)

David may have been a man after God's own heart in many areas, but he failed as a father. David's son, Amnon, raped his own half-sister. His son Absalom killed Amnon, tried to take the kingdom away from David, and even slept with David's concubines. David's son Adonijah tried to take the kingdom from David when the time for David to appoint his successor was near. David's family was a mess.

While it is certainly true that many of David's dysfunctional family problems likely resulted from his sin with Bathsheba, it is also pointed out that David had never interfered with Adonijah. It's quite probable that the same is true of his other children. He didn't even interfere enough to ask, "Why do you act like that?"

In football, interference is when a receiver is about to catch the ball and the defender cheats to prevent that from happening. He grabs, trips, blocks or does anything he can to keep the receiver from doing what he is planning to do – namely, catch the ball.

In sports this is illegal. But in parenting, this is critical. We must interfere and keep our kids from running free from our authority. And we need to do it with the fervency of a football player. The ball is in the air, the play is in progress, and we need to do anything and everything within our power to interfere with the lives of our children. Any tool is at your disposal: discipline, lectures, hard work, grounding, pulling them from school, banning them from bad influences, cutting off the T.V. Any of that is fair game if needed. When the game is on the line, big plays need to be made. An athlete will do whatever it takes to win. As parents we need to do the same, if not more. If we do not interfere, we will lose the game. If we do not interfere, our children will develop into wild and godless people like Adonijah, Absalom, and Amnon.

We must interfere for the good of our children! May we not be guilty of taking a hands-off approach to parenting!

An athlete will do whatever it takes to win. As parents we need to do the same, if not more.

What the Bible Says about Discipline

The Bible says that, "If you love your children, you will be prompt to discipline them." (Proverbs 13:24b NLT) This runs contrary to how many parents view discipline. Some people think discipline is mean or heartless. While this is understandable, it is a shortsighted view of discipline. Discipline is for a child's good, not harm. It may be painful or unpleasant for a short time, but in the end it brings about changes in a child's life that are good for him. That is why it is loving.

When a dentist drills into my tooth to remove decay, he is not being mean. He is putting me through discomfort, but it is for my own good. While it would be easy to view him as being unkind or even cruel, the reality is that he has devoted himself to a compassionate and caring profession. In the same way, when administered correctly, a parent's discipline is very loving.

The Bible also says that there is hope in discipline. Many parents feel hopeless in parenting. They are forever at the end of their patience, and they feel that the outcome of their parenting is no more guaranteed than the outcome of flipping a coin. Proverbs 19:18 says, "Discipline your son, for in that there is hope; do not be a willing party to his death." Discipline brings hope because it corrects the natural direction of a child's life and his natural inclination to take the path of destruction. There is a light at the end of the tunnel! There is a return here on the earth for all of your hard work! What do you think the verse means when it says, "Do not be a willing party to his death"? If you recall, in the case of Eli's sons, their unrestrained sin led, quite literally, to their deaths. The same might be said of David's sons Amnon, Absalom, and Adonijah. Proverbs 19:18 could also be a little more figurative and might be translated as "Do not let them destroy themselves" (NCV) or "If you don't, you will ruin their lives" (NLT). However you want to translate it, one thing is clear: parenting is serious business, and biblical discipline offers much hope in what could otherwise be a grave situation.

The Bible also says that disciplining your child can bring peace and delight to your soul.

> Proverbs 29:17 Discipline your son, and he will give you peace; he will bring delight to your soul.

Have you ever been frustrated with your kids? Are you at your wit's end at times? Has the thought: "Now I understand how child abuse happens," ever crossed your mind? I'm sure most of us can relate to those feelings. Parenting can get pretty stressful at times. Just as the sight of a boat gives hope to a castaway, or the sight of an oasis gives hope to a desert wanderer, discipline is the hope of a parent. If you are helpless, wearied, beaten down, haggard, frazzled, fried, and fatigued by your kids, you need discipline. Discipline restores peace to a home. Even a parent who has started to dislike his own children can turn the corner by bringing discipline into the home. God says that your child can even become a delight to your soul, so that the thought of him does not bring frustration and stress but pleasure and enjoyment.

Even though discipline brings many benefits like hope, peace, and delight, let's not miss the bigger picture. God is directing you to discipline your children. He is not throwing it out as an option and giving you a few reasons to consider whether or not you want to take His advice. The three passages we just looked at could be abbreviated to the following directives: "Be prompt to discipline," "Discipline your son," and again, "Discipline your son." Discipline is not optional; it is commanded. Remember Eli? His failure to discipline his children was not overlooked. He was punished severely for failing to follow God's direction in this.

While we certainly don't have perfect kids, we have reaped the benefits of discipline. Our home is peaceful, our children's behavior is a delight to us, and we are hopeful for the future of our kids. As we've loved our kids enough to shape and train them, we've found that it really works. Imagine that! God's way is the best way.

What Is Discipline?

So what is discipline? Rick Whitney, author of *Growing up Whitney*, puts it this way: "What do I mean by discipline? 'No!'

is what I mean." That pretty much says it all. It is giving directives to our kids to shape and restrain them. It's the do's and don'ts and the enforcement of those instructions.

We discipline ourselves when we go on a diet, exercise program, or try to better ourselves in some way. When we tell ourselves "no," we are exercising self-control, or self-discipline. When we tell our kids "no," we are helping control or discipline them to do as they should.

You may have noticed that "Discipline" and "Disciple" have the same roots. That is because they go hand-in-hand. A disciple is disciplined, and discipline is a form of training, or discipleship.

As you know, self-discipline is a character trait that impacts nearly every area of our moral fiber. Kids are sorely lacking in self-discipline. When kids are little, most of their good choices are imposed upon them. However, when they have been fully trained, or discipled, then they will impose the boundaries you have given them upon themselves. That is our ultimate goal in discipline.

Luke 6:40 A student is not above his teacher, but everyone who is fully trained will be like his teacher.

FROM OUR HOME

By the Seat of Her Pants

When Hope was little, long after the infamous laundry basket incident, she was out of bed when she wasn't supposed to be. We heard the noises of a child playing coming from her room and went to investigate. Sure enough there she sat on a cardboard apple box that was sitting near the head of her bed. She was desperately trying to scurry back into bed, but she couldn't seem to free herself from the box. Upon further investigation we found that when she sat on the box a chunk of her diaper slipped between the slits in the lid of the box.

We could hardly control our laughter as we realized the alarm she must have felt as she tried to escape our approaching footsteps only to find that the harder she pulled, the harder the box latched onto her.

Our kids are sure to make some wrong choices when our backs are turned. There is not much we can do about that, but we can pray. We know a mom that prays that her children's sins will catch up with them. God can help them get caught so that they don't start holding onto patterns of sin that never get addressed. We take courage in the idea that, just like Hope couldn't escape her predicament, there will be other times in our kids' lives when God will bring their sin to our attention.

> *Numbers 32:23 "But if you fail to do this, you will be sinning against the LORD; and you may be sure that your sin will find you out."*

To Spank or Not to Spank

Should you spank? Maybe it would be better if we could first talk about politics or war or something a little less controversial. This is a difficult subject because people come into it with so many preconceived notions of what spanking is. Some have been abused, some have seen abuse, some have heard of abuse, and some might even think that they have leanings toward being abusive. In such cases, it is certainly understandable that you may have vowed never to spank your children or may be repulsed by the mere consideration of the topic.

Most parents believe in spanking when the "crime" is serious enough – playing in the street, sticking paperclips in an outlet, and the like. Certainly such things ruin lives. But think of all the people you've ever known. How many have had their lives ruined by such events? You may know one or two, but most people have their lives ruined by behaviors that are just as destructive, but far more subtle. Rebellion is the big one. A kid who says "no" or defies parental instruction needs a spanking just as much, if not more, than a kid who plays with an outlet. We must see that defiance is far more likely to ruin lives than accidental tragedy—not to downplay basic household safety, but simply to underscore the things that far more commonly ruin kids.

Prisons are not full of people who like to run in the street (although I'm sure they'd like to if they could). They are not full of people jumping on their beds, sticking things into outlets or doing foolish things that could lead to physical harm. They are full of people who have no self-control—people who steal, kill, rob, rape, embezzle, and things of that sort. They came to a life-changing decision, a crossroads, and they made the wrong choice. For most of them, they've made that wrong choice time after time. Many of them are dead—not physically, but spiritually.

With discipline we have a hope of changing such behaviors and actually helping change the futures of our children. Of course, many people will wonder if we must spank to achieve these results, so we'll spend some time studying out this topic.

Let's start with some basics here. God is good, right? And He loves us, right? When God gives us direction in an area, it is for our own good, right? So, if God directs us to do something that seems wrong to us, something must be incorrect in our understanding of what God wants, or in our understanding of what we think is wrong. In other words, if we think it is wrong to spank, and if God directs us to spank, then either we are misunderstanding His direction to spank, or spanking is not a really a bad thing after all.

Please read through the following verses and ponder what you think God is saying.

Proverbs 13:24 He who spares the rod hates his son, but he who loves him is careful to discipline him.

Proverbs 23:13-14 Do not withhold discipline from a child; if you punish him with the rod, he will not die. Punish him with the rod and save his soul from death.

Proverbs 22:15 Folly is bound up in the heart of a child, but the rod of discipline will drive it far from him.

Proverbs 29:15 The rod of correction imparts wisdom, but a child left to himself disgraces his mother.

The use of "the rod," "the rod of discipline," and "the rod of correction" is what I'm going to refer to as spanking. As I'll address later on, there is no reason to take these verses as anything but literal. From these verses, is it clear to you that the Bible teaches the practice of spanking? It should be, because these are clear and straightforward verses. If this is offensive to you, then I challenge you to reconsider your position. Is it possible that spanking is a good, loving, and biblical practice? Could it be that the 5,000 year old wisdom given here is better than the advice of many present-day psychologists? I understand that some people's blood may be boiling by now, but hang with me here. These verses should be enough to make you at least pause and reflect on the possibility that spanking is part of God's good plan.

I suppose it would be wise at this point for some general guidelines that define biblical spanking. I'll address some of these more in depth later.

- Swats to the bottom, never to the face or body
- No hitting, beating, or kicking
- Controlled—not done in anger, but out of love
- Use of a small rod, not a hand
- Used to inflict a temporary sting, not damage
- Age appropriate

When spanking is done within these guidelines, it is loving (Proverbs 13:24), it is safe (Proverbs 23:13,14), and it is effective (Proverbs 22:15; 29:15). If a loving, safe, and effective form of discipline does not fit within your notion of what you believe is best for your children, then you need to stop and question your own motives. I'm not questioning if you love your children—not at all. But I would like to question if there is some roadblock that is keeping you from following God's wisdom and directives in this. Do you trust the latest magazine over God's Word? Are you withholding this form of discipline out of fear, instead of, in faith, trusting that God's way is best? Please give consideration to these questions as you read on and see what the Bible says about discipline. Since this is such a volatile topic, let's address some of the common questions and fears people have regarding spanking.

Is Spanking Abuse?

I once heard pastor John Meyer addressing the issue of discipline and in a strong tone he said something to the effect of, "Every night I pull down my son's pants and I hurt him on the bottom." A heavy silence fell on the room as we all wrestled with his statement in our minds. Even though he was a trusted friend and mentor I must admit that the doubts and questions started to race through my mind as well. Does he really do that *every* night? What if his son doesn't need discipline? Does he do it anyway? Why did he use the word "hurt"? Sure, spankings are painful, but the intent is not to hurt…well, at least that's not the chief goal. Finally he interrupted our thoughts with the words, "My son is diabetic, and I give him a shot of insulin."

I will never forget that illustration. It taught me two things. First of all, I (like many of us) can be quick to judge and to assume the worst about other people. Secondly, while introducing pain into someone's life might seem mean and cruel, there are times when it is necessary to do so for a greater good.

We don't think twice about giving a shot on the bottom. I think most of us would prefer a spank to a shot, so I think they are at least somewhat comparable. Yet we can tend to cringe at the idea of spanking. Why is that? Aren't both done for the wellbeing of the child?

What constitutes abuse?

I saw a woman split another woman wide open with a knife. The ensuing wound was at least a foot long. Blood was everywhere. One woman was having a C-section and the other was her doctor. Is that abuse?

There was a man that I saw force other men to manual labor until they were throwing up. Even then, he kept making them work. I saw this happen in the movie *The Miracle* which chronicled the achievements of the 1980 U.S. hockey team. The "manual labor" was when the coach made the team skate back and forth until it seemed as if they would die. Is that abuse?

Clearly, abuse cannot be simply defined as causing pain to another person. The intent of the action is a far greater indicator of what constitutes abuse. If you stick live electrical wires on someone because you think it is funny, that is a totally different thing from using shock paddles to jumpstart someone's heart. In fact, doctors and nurses have done all sorts of weird things to me that I'd rather not mention, but they do those things for my long-term benefit. If anyone else did those things for any other reason, I'd be tempted to sue. All summer long I hurt my kids by poking them with needles and knife blades, but I was not trying to be mean, I was just trying to take out splinters. It's better to face a little pain now than a great deal of pain later. This is an important principle to understand when it comes to discipline!

> *It's better to face a little pain now than a great deal of pain later.*

Personally, I think most doctors, coaches, and parents have their patients', athletes', and children's best interest in mind when they introduce pain into their lives. Certainly some are abusive. A few years ago I read an article about a doctor who carved his initials into his patient's stomach. Such an action is abusive and he should pay dearly for abusing the authority that was entrusted to him. But most surgeons are not abusive, and I certainly wouldn't recommend forbidding surgery. In the same way, I'd say that abuse against children is an atrocity, and parents that are abusive should be held accountable to an extreme level. **However, to equate spanking with abuse is an error. Spanking is a loving form of discipline that helps a child turn from harmful behaviors.**

Proverbs 13:24 He who spares the rod hates his son, but he who loves him is careful to discipline him.

Does Spanking Breed Violence?

One of the most common objections people have against spanking is that they are afraid it will make their kids hit other children and act out violently. In fact, almost all articles you read that are opposed to spanking will mention this concern, almost as if it is a well documented fact of science that spanking breeds violence.

There are some studies that link spanking with violence (as well as some that don't), but as we all know, such studies can be seriously flawed. Here are some questions that should be asked of studies on spanking. Do they separate spanking from beating? Do they consider age appropriateness? What is considered violence? A person who was spanked as a child is more likely to spank as an adult; does that automatically put that parent in the violent category, thus proving that spanking breeds violence? I had a teacher who said he was hit with a hammer as a child. Does he fall in the same statistical category as a child who is spanked with a wooden spoon? Do the researchers have agendas that might skew their approach to their research?

Since we usually don't know the answers to these questions when we hear different studies being quoted, let's consider a few common sense approaches to this question.

First of all, what is your experience? It is harder to capture what is really going on in a home on a survey than it is by observation. Are there some families you know that use spanking as a loving and healthy form of discipline? If so, what are their kids like? Are they the playground bullies? Do they hit other children? My own observation is this: children that are lovingly disciplined and spanked are far less violent than their non-spanked counterparts. Of course, I'd say that abused kids are the most violent. My kids have been spanked many times, yet it is extremely rare for them to act violently. In my personal experience, there is absolutely no connection between spanking and violence. None.

A second consideration is societal trends. Spanking is looked upon with more and more disfavor in our society. It is certainly less popular now than it was in the days of our grandparents. A question to consider is whether society is getting more violent, or less violent. If spanking greatly contributes to violence, and if, in our society, the frequency of spanking is greatly reduced, then it stands to reason that as a society the level of violence should be dropping as well. I realize that numerous other factors may play a part in societal violence, and that I am not providing you with any hard data. However, I still think it is a valid point to consider in a society that seems to be rapidly spinning out of control—particularly when it comes to teen violence and rebellion. Certainly spanking cannot be the evil atrocity that society says it is. Perhaps our grandparents were a little wiser and more civilized than we give them credit for being.

A third consideration is to reevaluate the initial premise. The basic idea is that spanking is violent, and therefore will breed violence. While at face value this may seem reasonable, let's think through another scenario using the same logic. Let's take kissing for example. Will kissing your children make them sexually promiscuous later in life? Perhaps it will make them incestuous, or maybe they will become pedophiles. I'm sure you see the fallacy in these ridiculous assertions. Obviously there is healthy kissing that promotes love and warmth in the relationship, and there is sexual kissing, which would be harmful for a child. To equate the two and to attribute the outcome of one form to another would be a serious flaw in logic. The same is true of discipline. There are healthy forms of corporal punishment and there are unhealthy forms. No one will argue against the fact that physical abuse will harm children in numerous ways, including making them more prone to being abusive. However, biblical spanking is not physical abuse. It causes no injury, it is not done in rage, and it is an act of love, not violence. To put spanking on the same level as violence is simply not a fair comparison.

A final consideration is the fact that the Bible teaches it. Did God in His infinite wisdom somehow miss the harms of spanking that our modern day researchers have now discovered? That is impossible! God knows what is best for our kids. It would be wise to trust Him over our modern day "experts." Regardless of all arguments for and against it, God's direction on the topic should be enough.

Would Jesus Spank?

We once had someone walk out of church when we were doing a parenting series. Even before the sermon started he looked over the handout and saw that we believed in biblical spanking. As he was leaving, he asked the question, "Would Jesus Spank?" I'm not sure I'd ever heard that question before, but it does capture some of the misconceptions about spanking. I did not talk to him and do not want to put words into his mouth, but here are some of my guesses as to what he was thinking:

- Spanking is not loving; and Jesus is.
- Spanking is painful; and Jesus wouldn't hurt anyone.
- Spanking harms children; and Jesus loved children.

I think all of these misconceptions stem from the belief that spanking is not loving. Before addressing spanking, we first need to grasp that discipline is a loving thing to do.

Revelation 3:19a [Jesus said,] "Those whom I <u>love</u> I rebuke and discipline."

Hebrews 12:5b "The Lord disciplines those He <u>loves</u>, and He punishes everyone He accepts as a son,"

Hebrews 12:5b is a quote from the following verse:

Proverbs 3:12 "...The LORD disciplines those He <u>loves</u>, as a father the son he delights in."

Proverbs 13:24 "He who spares the rod hates his son, but he who <u>loves</u> him is careful to discipline him."

Notice that the last verse shows that discipline is loving, *even when it involves spanking.* While all forms of discipline can be abusive when misused, God clearly views some forms of discipline as loving, and spanking is included as one of those forms.

You may wonder why that last verse says that "He who spares the rod hates his son." It reminds me of when Jesus said, "Which of you, if his son asks for bread, will give him a stone? Or if he asks for a fish, will give him a snake?"[35] Wouldn't a loving parent do loving things for his child? When we withhold good from our children, it is an act of unkindness. Discipline is a good thing, and when we withhold proper discipline, it is an unloving thing to do. The Bible clearly teaches that the loving thing is not to withhold spankings, but to spank.

So what about the question of spanking being painful? It is true that spanking is painful, at least for a time. Hebrews 12:11 says, "No discipline seems pleasant at the time, but painful." Discipline is painful, in all forms. Spanking may be physically

---

[35] Matthew 7:9-11

painful, but it is emotionally painful to get time-outs, a scolding, or losing privileges. While we could argue about which is more painful, the fact is, my kids would prefer to get a spanking and get it over with quickly. They would choose physical discipline every time. I'm not saying every kid is the same. I'm just saying that I wouldn't be overly fearful of how painful a loving and controlled spanking is.

The second part of the verse I just mentioned says, "Later on, however, it produces a harvest of righteousness and peace for those who have been trained by it." A harvest only comes after much planting. Typically, planting involves long hours, loss of sleep, and an investment of resources. I suppose you could say that is a painful process, but come harvest time, the focus is not on the painful process of planting, but it is on the joys of harvesting. Discipline is painful in different ways to both children and parents, but it produces a harvest. That harvest makes the pain endured or inflicted worthwhile. In the same way, studying is painful, but graduating is pleasant. Getting out of bed is painful, but being productive is not. Lifting weights is painful, but being strong is not. As we've already discovered, the result of our efforts makes the process worthwhile, even if the process is painful.

You may wonder whether I'm saying that the end justifies the means. No, I am not. The means are justified, not by the ends, but by the instruction given in the Bible. We do not spank because it works (which it does), but because that is what God says to do. But what I *am* trying to say is that the process is a good (though painful) process. It is not mean, but loving.

So would Jesus inflict pain on someone? That would be a great question to ask the money changers He chased out of the temple with a hand-made whip,[36] the Pharisees He gave

[36] John 2:14-16

a verbal beating to,[37] or Peter when Jesus said to him, "Get behind me Satan."[38] To me, those all seem like some pretty painful situations. Where we get confused is that we don't see those as painful *and* loving. It was loving to correct the money changers, to reprove the Pharisees, and to set Peter straight. It would have been unloving of Jesus to have let those people continue in their ways. When done correctly, a rebuke or a spank is painful *and* loving.

Many people also wonder if spanking is harmful to children. By now you probably realize that it is not harmful, but helpful. That's why God so often refers to discipline and love, not as opposing ideas, but as principles that go hand-in-hand.

In 2 Samuel 7:14, in reference to Solomon, God said, "I will be his father, and he will be my son. When he does wrong, I will punish him with the rod of men, with floggings inflicted by men." In this passage God clearly saw spanking as the common form of discipline used by fathers, and He said that He would treat Solomon with the same form of discipline. Yet He is calling Solomon His son out of love. In fact, in the next verse He says, "My love will never be taken away from him", and if you look into it a little further you'll find that Solomon's other name, Jedidiah, actually means 'loved of the LORD'.[39] I also like how in Proverbs 3:12 it says, "The LORD disciplines those He loves, as a father the son *he delights in.*" Godly discipline is not done to those we hate, but to those we delight in. Again, biblical discipline and love are clearly inseparable.

Look at the following passage. What does it say to you about love and discipline? What does it say about God's heart toward us as He disciplines, and about a father's heart toward his child?

---

[37] Matthew 23:1-39
[38] Matthew 16:23
[39] 2 Samuel 12:25

Hebrews 12:5-11 And you have forgotten that word of encouragement that addresses you as sons: "My son, do not make light of the Lord's discipline, and do not lose heart when He rebukes you, because the Lord disciplines those He loves, and He punishes everyone He accepts as a son." Endure hardship as discipline; God is treating you as sons. For what son is not disciplined by his father? If you are not disciplined (and everyone undergoes discipline), then you are illegitimate children and not true sons. Moreover, we have all had human fathers who disciplined us and we respected them for it. How much more should we submit to the Father of our spirits and live! Our fathers disciplined us for a little while as they thought best; but God disciplines us for our good, that we may share in His holiness. No discipline seems pleasant at the time, but <u>painful</u>. Later on, however, it produces a harvest of righteousness and peace for those who have been trained by it.

Note that the passage starts by stating that it is a "word of encouragement" and that it is because of God's love that He disciplines. It clearly states that discipline is painful; yet it is explained as a natural and loving process for our good.

So back to our original question, "Would Jesus spank?" I typically would not be so bold as to answer for Jesus as to what He would do or not do in a hypothetical situation. However, in this case I have no doubt. Jesus would spank. He would spank because it is loving, because it produces a harvest of righteousness, and because it protects children. It is also what the Bible clearly says to do, and Jesus would do it for that reason alone.

John 14:31 [Jesus said,] "...I love the Father. I do exactly what my Father has commanded me..."

How Can Outward Pain Cause Inward Change?

Some might question whether or not a spanking actually has any effect on the inside of a child? Doesn't it just change their outward behavior? Can we have any confidence that it changes the heart? That is a good question to ask. As parents, we really want our kids' hearts to change. It's great if their outward behavior changes, but we also understand that there are deeper problems than actions. What we'd really like to do is change the way they see things, the way they think, the way they process the world. Their hearts and minds must change, not just their actions.

To be honest with you, I do not understand how discipline changes the heart, but I know it does. I know it from experience in my family, and I know it from the Word. Proverbs 20:30 says, "Physical punishment cleanses away evil; such discipline purifies the heart." (NLT) Think about that for a second. Discipline does not just change actions, but it cleanses away evil. One version says that it "scours away evil."[40] Did you ever wish you could take some of the bad attitudes of your child and scrub them right off? That is what discipline does. Again, I do not understand the workings of this process, but it is true.

The second part of the verse really hits the nail on the head. "Discipline purifies the heart." Different translations render it as saying that it purges the inmost being, it reaches the inmost parts, and that it even changes an evil heart. That is significant. It is not superficial at all; instead, it is intensely deep and impacting.

Have you ever read Proverbs? It is full of God-given

[40] NAS

sayings of wisdom. As such, it often contrasts foolishness and wisdom.

Over 30 times it refers to fools and foolishness. For example, Proverbs 17:25 says, "A foolish son brings grief to his father and bitterness to the one who bore him."

Over 90 times it refers to wisdom with sayings such as, "Wisdom is supreme; therefore get wisdom. Though it cost all you have, get understanding."[41]

One might ask, "How can I help my kids to be wise?" I don't want to oversimplify this, but one way that foolishness is driven out is through spanking, and one way that wisdom is imparted is through spanking.

Carefully read the following verses:

Proverbs 22:15 Folly is bound up in the heart of a child, but the rod of discipline will drive it far from him.

Proverbs 29:15 The rod of correction imparts wisdom, but a child left to himself disgraces his mother.

Obviously you'll want to mix prayer, teaching, and training in there, but don't ignore the principle here! Spanking a child changes him on the inside. It cleanses away evil, it changes the heart, it drives out folly, and it imparts wisdom. Proverbs 23:14 even says that it could "save his soul from death." Whether that is a physical, spiritual, or even a figurative death, it is something from which I'd like to save my kids.

---

[41] Proverbs 4:7

Time-outs

By now I'm sure many people are wondering, "What about time-outs?"

The reason we use spanking as our main form of discipline for preteens is because that is what God recommends, and because He attaches promises to it. Maybe time-outs are somewhat effective, maybe they aren't. I doubt that they impart wisdom, or that they drive out folly. I suspect that they don't help in saving a soul from death, but I don't know for sure. Many forms of loving discipline, used consistently, will produce some good results. However, the first and best method for parents to use is spanking, because that is the form of discipline that God has recommended and the form to which He has attached promises.

Another reason I do not prefer time-outs is because they draw out the punishment. Ecclesiastes 8:11 says, "When the sentence for a crime is not quickly carried out, the hearts of the people are filled with schemes to do wrong." When a child is sent to her room or put into a corner, much of that time is spent with the child having an unchanged, unrepentant heart. It is better to deal with it swiftly than to leave her sulking. Give her a spanking, an explanation, a hug and move on. Why drag it out?

It also seems that many new offenses can occur during the time-out that typically go unaddressed, or get dealt with vaguely by having more time added. For example, while the child is standing in the corner she may use angry speech, step out of the corner, or may throw a fit. And what do you do with the child who just simply refuses to stay in the time-out? While these actions can accompany any form of discipline, spanking provides a clearer opportunity to discipline each infraction of the rules in a distinct and succinct manner.

While most parents would not intend this to be the case, time-outs can also communicate that the parent cannot tolerate being around the misbehaving child. As the child grows she may project that onto God and feel that when she does wrong there is a break in her relationship with God. A spanking communicates more clearly that the parent's love is still the same. The child is still accepted, but she must be corrected.

Natural Consequences

Another common form of discipline is the use of natural consequences. The basic idea is to figure out what the eventual consequences for a given action are, and then let those play out, or implement a similar punishment. For instance, if a child leaves an expensive toy outside by the street, that is irresponsible. The natural consequence for that irresponsibility would be for the toy to get stolen or damaged. So, if the toy gets stolen, then so be it. Your job is done. If the toy does not get stolen, then you could take away the toy for a lengthy period of time to simulate the natural consequence of having the toy stolen.

In sixth grade I had a teacher who took an envelope of money he found laying out with the word 'MONEY' written on it. I'm sure I remember the incident because the girl who lost the money blamed me for taking it. The reason she blamed me was because when she asked who took her money, I started smiling in an ornery sort of way. There was no reason for me to smile. I hadn't taken the money and had no idea that the teacher had. I don't know why I do that, but guilty or innocent, I've always had a hard time keeping a straight face. Anyway, after letting her accuse me for a bit, the teacher told her that I was innocent, and that he, in fact, had taken the money. He used the event to teach her not to leave money lying around, not to write "MONEY" on an envelope containing it, and not to accuse someone falsely. It was a very effective lesson. Almost 30 years later I still remember it. It was a good use of natural consequences as a way of teaching a lesson.

Natural consequences can be an excellent form of discipline on occasion, especially as children get older and can understand and experience the consequence in a significant way and not just a superficial way. Such lessons can effectively bring home a point in an impacting way. However, I don't find the use of natural consequences to be practical with younger children in most situations. In fact, I often find them to be just plain confusing.

What is the natural consequence of a two-year-old grabbing another kid's juice off the table? Well, I suppose she could spill it all over herself. You'd tend to think that that would be uncomfortable and would make her want to stop getting drinks off the table, but some two-year-olds don't seem terribly bothered by getting a wet shirt. In fact, it may even add to the joys of exploring and experimenting. In any case, it doesn't seem like I should go ahead and pour the juice on her to simulate the natural consequence. I suppose another consequence is that we'd run out of juice earlier. So we could withhold her drink at the next meal, but I doubt a two-year-old is going to connect with that. She may not even notice if she gets milk or water instead. I suppose we could withhold all drinks, but the most likely natural consequence of that is a whole bunch of fussing. I suppose cleaning up the mess is a natural consequence. Although, it is possible that she succeeded in getting the drink without spilling it. In that case, she would still need to be disciplined for not obeying.

I do not think this is simply a difficult example because I am talking about a two-year-old. What is the natural consequence when your son forgets to take out the trash? I suppose you could pile all the trash in his bedroom. You could make him pay the electric bill when he leaves the fridge door open too long, or you could dry out the toothpaste in the oven when he leaves the cap off.

I do think natural consequences are valuable to some extent, but here are the concerns I would have with using them exclusively, or even primarily, with young children:

1) When parents focus on natural consequences it can be easy to overlook the aspect of rebellion. When a child stays up 5 minutes past lights-out, the issue is not that he is going to lose 5 minutes worth of sleep and be that much more tired the next day. The issue is that he refused to comply with a simple standard that you asked of him. The issue is rebellion, not sleepiness.

2) As I already mentioned, natural consequences can make a simple issue of discipline confusing. If they did wrong, discipline them for their wrong. There does not always have to be an ideologically perfect sentence for the crime. Consistency is more important than creativity.

3) The real beauty of natural consequences is that they are natural. When a child loses $5 on a bet, that $5 is gone and it can't be used for buying something that the child wants. Natural consequences happen naturally, so parents should not have to rack their brains to come up with them.

4) Strong proponents of natural consequences can make it seem as if any non-consequence-related discipline is ineffective. My only detention ever was at the hands of that same sixth grade teacher. I got up to sharpen my pencil at an inappropriate time and he slapped a detention on me. (Obviously, I was an evil child.) While the lesson about the envelope made an impression on me, so did the detention. One was a natural consequence and one was not. Both served a purpose; both were effective. The point is that there *are* undoubtedly forms of discipline other than natural consequences that are effective.

5) The benefit of other forms of discipline is that they bring consequences more rapidly, and in a more controlled manner. What is the natural consequence for a boy who scales the big climbing tree a little too high? It seems like it would be to break his arms and legs. I do not want to wait until my children learn this lesson through natural consequences, and I would certainly not break his limbs to teach him the lesson! Instead, I introduce the unnatural consequence of a spanking, which teaches that disobeying your parents brings unpleasant consequences. And that is a lesson that has value not just for scaling trees, but for numerous life situations.

> *Be careful to emphasize the methods that the Bible clearly emphasizes, and deemphasize those that it does not.*

6) Everyone faces natural consequences all the time, and yet we still struggle to do right. There are plenty of 60-year-olds who are criminals, even though they have had a lifetime of natural consequences from which to learn. We often need more than that. That is why God has given authority to governments, and they give us tickets when we speed or even park illegally. That helps us to keep in line with what is good and right. That is also why He gives authority to parents.

7) As with time-outs, we do not have the biblical promises attached to natural consequences. Will they drive out folly and impart wisdom, or change the heart? There are no guarantees.

Again, I do think there is value in using natural consequences in some situations, but I don't think they should be a replacement for spanking. They should not be a substitute. It is important for children to learn the consequences of their actions, but much of that can be done verbally, or during sporadic times when the opportunity presents itself. Using natural consequences is not wrong. It is a great thing. However, I'd be careful to emphasize the methods that the Bible clearly emphasizes, and deemphasize those that it does not.

When to Start Discipline

Humans have been given the five senses of touch, taste, smell, sight, and hearing. These senses help us interact with our environment. They can help lead us to what is pleasurable, enjoyable, or good for us, or they can help steer us away from things that are poisonous, or harmful. If we perform an action and our senses signal back to our brain to tell it that the action produced an unpleasant result, then we are much less likely to repeat that same action.

If you grab a cactus, your sense of touch tells you not to do that again. If you take a big whiff of a smelling salt, your sense of smell tells your brain not to do that again. If you put a microphone in front of a speaker and cause feedback, your sense of hearing tells you to stop. If you hastily grab a glass of milk and spill it all over, your sense of sight lets you know to be more careful next time. If you take a big bite of spinach, your sense of taste tells your brain to spew it back out as quickly as possible. Okay, so the senses aren't always completely accurate, but they obviously serve the function of training you not to do what you shouldn't.

Even a young child operates in the same way. If she touches a plant and you say, "No," and gently slap her bottom or her hand, her sense of touch will inform her brain that touching plants causes an unpleasant reaction that should be avoided. Of course, she may test the theory a few times, just to be sure, but she will quickly make the connection and stop touching the plant, and eventually all plants.

There is no set age in the Bible as to when any particular form of discipline should be started, but spanking should be primarily for rebellion, and in order to rebel a child must have some comprehension of what the rules are. Romans 5:13 says that "sin is not taken into account when there is no law." With children, how can there be any law without an understanding of the law?

At what age this understanding develops is open to discussion, but I think a child is equipped to respond to simple cause-and-effect discipline by 7 or 8 months old. Obviously at that age you would want to be pretty gentle about it, but a gentle swat for touching plants or electrical cords and a firm "No!" should help them learn the meaning of "No" quite quickly. (If done carefully, these are not terribly painful. In fact, most of our babies laughed at first. They thought the whole interaction was humorous until about the third time.) When they can understand simple instruction like, "Shut the door" or "give me the bottle" they are able to process much more complicated information than "No" and should be disciplined more readily.

I'm sure the thought of disciplining such a cute little youngster will make many parents cringe, but we must understand that it is loving and it is immensely helpful in training children to be happy and obedient. As our babies start to crawl, we are already starting to define boundaries to help protect them, and to start developing their character.

How Pain Relates to Training

Many will wonder, "How in the world can I hurt my own child?" This is an understandable question, but we need to be careful not to get too caught up in the emotions of it. We all want what is best for our children, and we need to give strong consideration to just what is really the best. Certainly by now we all understand the need for some sort of discipline, and if you'll recall, Hebrews 12:11 says that, "No discipline seems pleasant at the time, but painful." Discipline is necessary and painful—in one way or another.

Obviously the *goal* of discipline is not to hurt our children; it is to help them. However, we need to consider not just the pain caused by discipline, but also that life will bring hurts into a person's life. All kinds of hurts exist. There are emotional hurts (like divorce), physical hurts (like car accidents), and spiritual hurts (like disappointment in God). Some hurts are unavoidable, but many of the hurts that come into our children's lives will be as a result of their own poor choices. If they are not well trained, the amount of pain that our children bring into their own lives will be greatly increased.

Perhaps it would be good for us to think through the tradeoff that occurs when we spare our children from painful discipline. Would you rather have your child hit by a car or spanked for running into the street? Would you rather have him take a bottle of pills or experience a little pain on the bottom for playing in the medicine cabinet? Would you rather have your child suspended from school for mouthing off to the principal or spanked several times throughout his life for talking back to you? Every time we discipline we are trying to prevent some future harmful form of disobedience. We don't know exactly what may happen, but we are training our children to help them avoid future unknown hurts in life. In other words, we are trading future hurts of unknown levels of pain and intensity for present hurts given in a loving and controlled environment.

We are trading future hurts of unknown levels of pain and intensity for present hurts given in a loving and controlled environment.

Many times parents will say that spanking does not work for them. Several different factors can make discipline ineffective, but one common reason is that they are doing it in such a way that it is not painful. If you know that doing something will cause you pain you will not do it. It is as simple as that. Pain is a natural teacher in that way. If you know that grabbing a hot pot off the stove will burn your hands, you will not do it. It's a pretty basic principle. If your child knows that talking back to you will definitely result in painful discipline, he will not do it (at least not very often). However, talking back yields some satisfaction for your child, so you've got that working against you. That being the case, the pain your child experiences needs to outweigh the pleasure that comes from the particular form of disobedience you are trying to correct. If the pain of discipline outweighs the pleasure associated with the disobedience, obedience is sure to follow. If training is not working, ask yourself, "Is it painful enough?"

Do not grieve that you are bringing physical pain into your child's life. You must see the benefit of it! You are saving your child from pain later in life. As the verse says, painful discipline will produce a harvest of right living (righteousness) and peace in your child's life. It may not seem pleasant to the child at the time, but the end result of it is pleasant.

At this point, let me reiterate how much we dearly love our kids. We would do anything for them. They bring us joy and delight. Most people have described our children as warm and pleasant. Please don't think that because we spank we must have had abnormally naughty children. On the contrary, our kids are generally obedient kids, but even good kids still need much training if we are going to shape them into something beyond their natural selves.

FROM OUR HOME

Immediate, Memorable, Consistent

A few years ago, when Hope was 8, she had a reading light next to her bed. It was missing a light bulb and she was examining what the socket looked like and felt like. It wasn't long before screams of terror were coming from her room. She had stuck her finger in the socket. It was quite a shocking event. (She didn't think I was funny either.)

She has never repeated this action, and she never will. I doubt that any of us will. She learned her lesson, and she learned it well. Why did she learn it so well? Electricity is an effective teacher because it is immediate, memorable, and consistent. Common sense will tell you that any discipline that is applied in a similar manner will also be effective.

1. **Immediate** – If a large chunk of fat bulged out of your body every time you ate a candy bar, you would stop eating candy bars. The immediacy of the consequence gives hesitation to the action. If you stick your finger in a socket you immediately know not to do that again.

2. **Memorable** – I've tested many 9-volt-batteries by sticking them to my tongue. The ensuing shock does not leave enough of an impression on me that it deters me from repeating the action. However, sticking your finger in a light socket is quite another matter. The light socket sends a painful message that says, "Don't even think about doing that again."

3. **Consistent** – Have you ever been caught in a downpour without an umbrella? If it rained every time you left the house you would not be found without one very often. In regions where storms are more consistent, so is the practice of carrying an umbrella. Every single time you touch two live wires you will get shocked. Electricity is very consistent. That is why we have a healthy fear of it.

All discipline that is immediate, memorable, and consistent will work.

Basics of Discipline

So far we've looked at the Scriptural basis for child training. I'd like to give some practical advice as to how to discipline. The Bible leaves much room on the specifics of discipline. I'm going to share some things that have worked for us, and you can pray about what you're going to implement and what you are not.

As I mentioned before, we start discipline when the kids are around eight months old. We start with light swats to the hand for touching forbidden objects like plants and outlets. The reason we swat their hands is because it makes an obvious connection to touching, and we want the correlation between their wrongful action and the swat to be very plain.

We say, "No touch," firmly and clearly and then we swat his hand. When he reaches to grab the object again we say "No" again and swat his hand again. A child at that age does not completely understand everything, but it does not take him long to realize that when we say "No," he had better stop what he is doing.

After saying "No" or after disciplining, we do not whisk the child away from the temptation or try to distract the child. We may say something like, "Choose something else to play with," but we do not avoid the confrontation. While this is the exact opposite of what many modern day parenting experts recommend, we hold firmly to the wisdom of this process. Our goal is not to simply get the child to not touch the object; our goal is to train the child to choose to yield and to listen to our instruction.

Even at this age a young child will have a will of his own and will push the limits just to make sure you are serious about what you said. We will continue this process until the child obeys. For the first few times, that may take several rounds, but the child usually quickly learns the cause and effect of touching plants and other forbidden objects.

Some people also teach that toddlers should be given total freedom to explore and to learn by touching and sticking things in their mouths. While I agree that exploration is an important part of the learning process and certainly would not forbid everything, I think one of the most valuable lessons in life is to learn to yield to authority. Yielding to the authority of parents, teachers, and policemen is great practice for yielding to the authority of God. Learning to yield is a more valuable lesson than the lesson of learning what a plant feels or tastes like.

When a child turns a year or so, we start swats to the bottom. By this time their comprehension is much greater, and they've certainly learned the cause and effect nature of their actions. Please understand that in all discipline we use simple commands and instructions that we are confident they are capable of understanding and obeying.

This may be initially disturbing to some of you, but we use a rod when we start swats to the bottom. There are a number of reasons people use to explain why using a rod is better than a hand, but the best reason is that the Bible repeatedly talks about the use of a rod. People obviously had hands back then, just as we do, but the Bible still talks about using a rod. Not one time does the Bible mention disciplining with the hand.

Proverbs 13:24 He who spares the rod hates his son, but he who loves him is careful to discipline him.

Proverbs 23:13-14 Do not withhold discipline from a child; if you punish him with the rod, he will not die. Punish him with the rod and save his soul from death.

Proverbs 22:15 Folly is bound up in the heart of a child, but the rod of discipline will drive it far from him.

Proverbs 29:15 The rod of correction imparts wisdom, but a child left to himself disgraces his mother.

Another reason often given for using a rod is the thought that in the child's mind the instrument of discipline becomes separated from the person giving the spanking.

Using a rod is also less likely to cause damage than using a hand. You don't have to use much force with a rod to inflict a good little sting, but with a hand you have to use considerably more force. This greatly increases the risk of hurting your child.

In the Hebrew a rod is a branch or a stick. Some authors say that means it is flexible; some say that it isn't. Personally, I don't believe that the point of the verses which mention a rod is the size, shape, and flexibility of the instrument of discipline. The emphasis of those verses is not the *type* of rod, but the *use* of the rod. Using the rod lovingly, consistently, and unsparingly will have a vastly greater impact than the use of a specific type of rod.

We usually use a rod in the form of a wooden spoon. I know the Bible doesn't talk about wooden spoons, but perhaps that is because they were difficult to make and they wanted to save them for cooking. Now they are cheap, dispensable, found in every kitchen, and are, amazingly, a lot like a rod. I don't understand the physics of it, but somehow the head of the spoon makes the spoon easier to aim.

Aim is important. If you miss the bottom and hit the back or upper legs you will know immediately by your child's cries that you went out of bounds. If you have a bad aim you may want to place a folded up towel over his back just in case you miss.

We usually try to take them to the bathroom to spank them, especially as they get older. We do this so that it is in a controlled and private environment. As adults we should correct one another privately, and we should give our kids the same privacy. Matthew 18:15a says, "If your brother sins against you, go and show him his fault, just between the two of you." Keep it just between the two of you.

We spank for blatant acts of disobedience. This is the common stated practice of most people who believe in spanking. However, we believe that blatant acts of disobedience occur all the time. Some people will only spank if the child does something really atrocious, and even then, only if he does it right after being told not to. We believe blatant acts of disobedience occur when a child lies, hits, deceives, or defies. Crossing boundaries we have set, throwing tantrums, being disrespectful or talking back will all potentially lead to a spanking. These are things we discuss with our children all the time, so there is no reason to chalk these actions up to forgetfulness or childishness. We know our kids and what we can expect from them. They can be held to a high standard.

While these standards combined with this level of spanking might make it sound like we don't do anything in our house except spank, the reality is that effective discipline leads to better behavior and less discipline. So while we may spank more than most when our kids are little, it is still pretty infrequent once our kids are well-trained.

These are some of the basics of discipline as lived out in our house. As parents we are responsible for the raising of our children, and you are responsible for yours. It doesn't matter whether or not you agree with our methods; you need to pursue God on this and figure out how you think He wants you to lead your family. Ask Him for wisdom and clarity.

Some Practical and Simple Commands

1) Look into my eyes.

Sometimes it can be confusing as to when a child is being defiant, or just childish. One way to tell if your child is being rebellious is by giving him a simple command that you know he understands. Suppose he knocks his cup off of the table and then, thirty seconds later, spills his whole bowl full of dry cereal all over the floor. Should you spank for that? Of course not, assuming it was an accident. But was it an accident?

In this situation I would say, "Look into my eyes." If he obeys by looking into my eyes, then it is likely that it was just an accident. Now, why would I say this? What kind of barometer is that, you ask?

Well, if he is actually being rebellious and defiant, then any command, no matter how simple, will be met with resistance. He will look out the window or even at my chin or forehead, but not at my eyes. He may even obey partly and turn his head toward me, but not his eyes. In our house this would be an immediate spanking. Why? Because we gave him a simple command that he understood (all our kids know this command well), and he refused to yield. What a great training opportunity it is to discipline in that type of environment rather than in a more serious situation, like when we say, "Don't go past the sidewalk." Occasionally issuing a simple heart-test command like this makes it easy to correctly discern an otherwise confusing situation. I call it a heart-test because I am doing

Occasionally issuing a simple heart-test command like this makes it easy to correctly discern an otherwise confusing situation.

something to find out where the heart is—a heart-test command.

2) Touch my leg.

Another heart-test command we issue is, "Come touch my leg." It is a simple and clear directive that you can tell was either obeyed, or it wasn't. If you just say, "Come here," and the child comes half way or three fourths of the way, did he obey? I don't know, because the instruction wasn't clear. But if you say, "Come touch my leg," and the child comes all the way but does not touch your leg, then he did not obey completely. Failure to obey would be a spank. I know you are thinking we are Nazis at this point, but you've got to understand that we are shooting for their hearts. Why shouldn't a simple command be completely obeyed? The reality is, if you are consistent with a few commands like these, they will rarely be challenged. The kids will obey completely and touch your leg every time. Such a response is so encouraging to a parent! It is frustrating when a child won't come at all or only comes half way!

3) Specific and simple

Exodus 20:8-11 "Remember the Sabbath day by keeping it holy. Six days you shall labor and do all your work, but the seventh day is a Sabbath to the LORD your God. On it you shall not do any work, neither you, nor your son or daughter, nor your manservant or maidservant, nor your animals, nor the alien within your gates. For in six days the LORD made the heavens and the earth, the sea, and all that is in them, but He rested on the seventh day. Therefore the LORD blessed the Sabbath day and made it holy."

See how God closes the loopholes on this command? If He had just said not to work, we'd have our kids work. If He had banned that, we would have had other people work for us. Had He banned that, we would have plowed our fields thinking "I'm really not working, my oxen are." God closed the loopholes.

Giving them specific instruction makes it easy to determine what level of obedience is truly obedience. For example, we've never had much success with telling young kids to "calm down." "Calming down" is vague and open to interpretation. Define it for them. What do you want? Try saying things like, "Don't talk, stop running, and quit touching the other kids." This is the type of clear and simple instruction that has worked well for us. Over time they need to learn what it means to calm down, but that is something that must be taught using more specific terms.

4) Say, "Yes, Dad."

One last practical heart-test that we ask our kids is to say "Yes, Mom" or "Yes, Dad." After we give a child instruction, we want him to acknowledge that he heard and understood. For instance, if I say, "Please stop running in the house", I want him to say, "Yes, Dad" because that lets me know that he heard and is planning to obey. If he does not say, "Yes, Dad", I usually prompt him for it. Again, this can be a simple heart-check command, and I expect it to be obeyed precisely. I did not ask him to say "Okay," "Just a second," "Yes," or "All right." I asked him to say "Yes, Dad."

It is also important that he uses the right tone. He may not answer in a begrudging or a you-are-so-unreasonable tone. If he does not respond in a respectful way, I may give him one more chance. "Say, 'Yes, Dad!'" and this time saying it as cheerfully as possible—a routine he recognizes and knows means he needs to imitate closely. If he still responds in a less than honoring tone, then he needs to be disciplined. Why? Because what I want is complete obedience, even at the heart level. If he says anything else, I will correct him for it.

Are we extreme, or what? Don't get me wrong; our home is not run in a rigid military style. However, we've found it useful to have a few basic family guidelines that can always act as heart-checks. We may show a little more grace with other instructions, but on these heart-check commands we are pretty inflexible, and this helps us maintain order without being oppressive. Our goal is not to produce little robots. Our goal is to develop God-followers—kids who wholeheartedly love God. Throughout this process we are always careful to capture their hearts, and not just their obedience, and we view discipline as a crucial part of this process.

Steps of Discipline

The following verse is a parenting gem. The passage was not given directly as parental advice, but it beautifully highlights some important steps of discipline. The Word is full of jewels that are helpful to parenting, marriage, and all areas of life.

> *2 Corinthians 2:6-11 The <u>punishment</u> inflicted on him by the majority is <u>sufficient</u> for him. Now instead, you ought to <u>forgive</u> and <u>comfort</u> him, so that he will not be overwhelmed by excessive sorrow. I urge you, therefore, to <u>reaffirm your love</u> for him.*

Notice the steps of discipline that are brought out by this verse:

1. Discipline sufficiently.

Discipline in a way that sufficiently teaches your child not to do wrong. Do not be too soft; do not be too harsh.

2. Forgive.

Once the act of discipline is over, make sure you have the child ask for forgiveness. Please understand that the parent is not asking for forgiveness for disciplining the child. The parent has done nothing wrong. The parent is reminding the child to ask for forgiveness from the parent and any other offended party. He needs to do this, as it is a significant part of making sure that he is repentant (2 Corinthians 7:10,11). Then say to your child, "I forgive you." The Bible says to "Forgive as the Lord forgave you" (Colossians 3:13). When He forgave you He did not keep rubbing your face in your sin, but He separated your sins from you as far as the east is from the west,[42] He took away your sins and washed you whiter than snow.[43] We need to grant our children complete forgiveness as well.

3. Comfort.

Give your child a hug or rub his back. Give him a short time to cry and to collect himself. If the adult in the above verse needs comfort, how much more so your child.

4. Reaffirm your love.

Tell your child that you still love him and that God still loves Him. He is a special person and God has special plans for his life.[44] That is why you are taking the effort to train him.

---

[42] Psalm 103:12
[43] Psalm 51:7
[44] Ephesians 2:10

Once you've done all of these steps, it is a done deal. The relationship is restored and you can go on completely at peace with one another. The child should not be bitter and crying uncontrollably, and the parent should not be angry. Typically there would not be a reason to bring up the incident again. It is all completely dealt with and life should go back to a completely united state.

Anger and Discipline

If you find yourself getting angry at your kids it is most likely because you are not disciplining them soon enough.

"Please turn the TV down...turn the TV down...I said, 'Please turn down the TV'...TURN THE TV DOWN RIGHT NOW...**DON'T MAKE ME COME DOWN THERE...**"

Have you ever done that? I know that I've been guilty of that at times. While I understand how easy it is for this to occur, that does not make it right. When you interact with your kids in this manner it shows that:

1) You are being lazy and selfish in your discipline by not disciplining sooner.

2) You have trained your kids that they don't have to obey until you get really mad.

Their continued disobedience is understandably incredibly frustrating, but let's face it, they are only doing the same thing most of us do. Do you drive the speed limit, or the enforced speed limit? Most of us will push the limit on boundaries. I try to be on time with all my bills, but I know if I'm late on my home owner's association dues they will fine me. On that bill I am especially careful to be on time. The point at which a rule is enforced is the point at which I tend to take the rule seriously.

If you had disciplined your child after the first time he did not obey, you could have done it while you were still calm, and you could have taught him to obey you on the first occasion.

Counting is similar. If they know that you will not discipline until you count to ten, that grants them a license to do wrong until you count to nine.

Of course it is always wise to work on your temper. Yet if you'll just be consistent in discipline, it should greatly reduce the frequency of frustrating situations that you experience in your parenting.

Proverbs 29:11 A fool gives full vent to his anger, but a wise man keeps himself under control.

Proverbs 14:29 A patient man has great understanding, but a quick-tempered man displays folly.

Psalms 4:4a In your anger do not sin.

Colossians 3:8 But now you must rid yourselves of all such things as these: anger, rage, malice, slander, and filthy language from your lips.

A parent who blows up at his child physically, verbally, or emotionally, is a parent who is disobeying God. Somehow, when we get angry it is easy to blame those we are angry with, but we have no right to anger. God did give us the rights and responsibilities of discipline, but He never gave us the authority to be abusive, either physically or verbally, with His children.

It's only natural for our kids to disobey at times. We must not take this personally. Instead, we need to calmly and lovingly direct them through discipline. The Word says that they have folly bound up in their hearts.[45] Folly and disobedience

---

[45] Proverbs 22:15

from our children should not surprise us. They are just doing what kids do; we just need to do what parents should do. There is no advantage to making a big deal out of it.

Children, even babies, are going to do things that are irritating. If God struck us with lightning every time we were irritating, I imagine our planet would look like a lunar landscape. God treats us with grace and mercy. God does discipline and correct us, but only in very rare, extreme situations does He just outright let someone have it. Over a dozen times the Bible says that God is slow to anger and abounding in love. We need to have this same heart toward our children.

Can Other Forms of Discipline Be Blessed?

At one of our parenting seminars someone asked the following question: *I wasn't raised being spanked, and I have never really believed in spanking. Can other forms of discipline be blessed?*

This is a question that is on the minds of many, so it is certainly worth looking into. Below is the response I wrote to the question:

There are certainly other forms of discipline that can be blessed. Rebuke is a clear biblical example of another form of discipline (Proverbs 9:8; 13:1; 17:10; 19:25). I'm not sure how old your kids are, but it is important to note that Scripture seems to imply that rebuke is for those who are older and wiser. Taking away privileges or adding work are forms of discipline that can also be effective and that can be backed biblically. For example, God added work to Adam when he sinned in the garden. God also took away a privilege from Moses when He prevented him from entering into the Promised Land.

Rather than expand on those thoughts, I'd like to take another angle on this question. When you ask if other forms can be blessed, it seems that you realize there is a blessing that comes with spanking. In other words, you seem to be saying that you realize that the Bible teaches spanking, and therefore God will bless it. However, for some reason you are reluctant to use it. Perhaps that is because of your own upbringing, negative accounts you've witnessed or read about, or maybe you are afraid that spanking may lead to abuse.

Let me ask you this question. Do you feel that God wants you to spank? This is an important question. Suppose you were a foster parent and were not allowed to spank, and wrote to ask if other forms could be blessed. I would say, "Absolutely!" In other words, if you were in a situation where spanking was prohibited, and you felt it would be honoring to God not to spank, I certainly believe God would bless you as you practiced other forms of biblical discipline. On the other hand, suppose you believe that spanking is biblical and that God wants you to spank, but you aren't willing to be obedient. I do not think God will bless in that situation.

For example, I do not believe God wants me to spank our children when they are infants and unable to understand instructions. Spanking is primarily for rebellion, and it is not possible to rebel against a rule without being able to comprehend what the rule is. Therefore I would not spank a 5-month-old. Although infants can certainly be fleshly, I'd say they are technically not rebelling because they can't comprehend the rules. I believe this is God's will in this matter; therefore, it would be wrong for me to spank an infant. (Of course, it would also be wrong for anyone else in this example.) I do believe God wants me to spank my 3-year-old. This is what God has directed in His Scripture, and I have no reason to believe that my situation is an exception to God's input in this area. Someone else may be in a different situation and believe God's will is different. He may have a 3-year-old whose mental progress is impaired. Or there could be a situation where a wife wants to spank, and her husband doesn't want her to. In these cases, and in any case, it is important to know and follow God's will.

Does that make sense? If you are seeking God's blessing, the way to get it is to follow God's will. If you know His will, or in other words, if you know what He wants you to do, then do that. It is ill-advised to do something other than God's will, and still hope that God will bless.

James 4:17 Anyone, then, who knows the good he ought to do and doesn't do it, sins.

I'd encourage you to reconsider trying to find another way to discipline. Instead, explore why you are holding to a position of not believing in spanking, when it is clearly taught in the Bible. Don't use your current thoughts on the matter as a starting point. Start from God's Word, and then follow God's instruction as He leads you. Do you have questions, concerns, and fears on this topic? Address those. Ask questions, study the Scripture, and get godly advice. Pray that God will reveal His will to you in this matter. James 1:5 says, "If any of you lacks wisdom, he should ask God, who gives generously to all without finding fault, and it will be given to him." When God answers your prayer, and you're confident that He has shown His will to you, then do His will. In James 1:22 it says, "Do not merely listen to the word, and so deceive yourselves. Do what it says."

What to Do When Discipline Isn't Working

Here are a few pointers on what to do if you feel like your discipline is not working. You are bound to feel this way at times, but you need to take heart! Don't get defeated. You can win with your child. Each one is different and some have more spunk and willpower than others. Parenting can get really hard at times, but you will win if you stick in there.

When things get difficult, make sure you get input from your small group leader or someone who is close to the situation. Ask them for open and frank input on all areas that relate to your parenting. Oftentimes it is easier for an outsider to see our issues than it is for us to see them ourselves.

Here are some basics I'd want to make sure you're confident in if things are getting really tough.

More love and relationship

Make sure you (both parents) are connected with your child. Are you in the home enough? Is she with sitters or in daycare frequently? I'd cut out as much of that as you can. She needs you.

Some kids like lots and lots of attention, and for some of them, negative attention seems better to them than minimal attention. Some kids will go through spankings just to get to the kiss and make-up part at the end. Make sure that throughout the day you are touching her, saying "I love you", and making eye contact with her when you talk to her.

More discipline

Kids will act up if they think they can win. Some kids will give up the battle of the wills if they have a ten percent chance of getting caught and/or disciplined. Although it's always best to be consistent, a little inconsistency with these kids might not be a real big deal.

However, all kids are different. Some kids feel victorious with far less. If they can win one battle out of twenty, then they consider that a victory. They will battle every time in hopes of winning just once. Losing nineteen battles is no big deal as long as they can win the twentieth. So, check your consistency level.

When you've been disciplining a child time after time, it can be easy to get fearful of entering into discipline situations. For some parents this can lead to weaker parenting. They make excuses for their children's misbehavior, accept less than complete obedience, and shy away from giving instructions that they worry might be disobeyed.

Here's an example:

"Gimme that toy. Give it right now... Hurry up... Okay, you want to put it on the chair? That's fine. But don't touch it again... I said, 'Don't touch it again'... Okay if you want to touch it that's fine, but you better not pick it up... Put that back down. If you don't put it down I'm going to tell your father..."

The child in that situation just won five battles. She didn't obey quickly. She put the toy in a place different than she was told to. She touched it again. She picked it up again. She didn't put it down again quickly.

I'd take the battle back to the first offense and discipline after she put the toy in the wrong place. Take away her victories. If she has no hope of winning such battles, there is no point engaging with you at that level.

I would also caution against getting fearful that something is terribly wrong with your child. I remember when we asked a pediatrician to check the hearing of one of our kids. A knowing smile came over his face as he obliged. Surprisingly, everything checked out just fine. I don't think we were the first parents to think our child couldn't hear. You see, the problem wasn't hearing, it was obeying.

We may be tempted at times to think our child must

have some physical problem, and more than a few parents have even wondered if their child was demon possessed. While we don't want to ignore the possibility of some sort of disability, there's a good chance that all that is wrong is that our child has a selfish, independent, and rebellious streak. Nothing personal, I'm just saying kids can be rebellious, and neither your child nor mine is exempt from that.

If she can obey sometimes, she can obey all the time.

I suppose it is possible that there are aspects of a child's disposition, psychological makeup, or physical health that make her more prone to rebellion, but that doesn't make it okay to be rebellious. If she can obey sometimes, she can obey all the time, or at least become a generally obedient child. Could she be more prone to acting up at times? Sure. I'm definitely grouchier when I'm tired, but I need to control that regardless of my vulnerability to it. She may be more sensitive to how much you are home, or things that are said to her, or to what she eats for breakfast. Sure, there could be contributing factors to when she struggles, but like all of us, she needs to learn to use self-control even when she is tired, sick, irritable, ticked off, or whatever.

More instruction

Give your young kids lots of structure. Kids thrive with structure. Have your child always operating under your direction. Practice 'blanket time' with her. Set her on a blanket for 30 minutes with 3 or 4 toys. Have her play quietly without getting off. Stay close to keep an eye on her.

If she fusses or gets off, discipline her for disobeying you. This will help her learn to obey your instructions and to stay within boundaries that you set for her.

If she was really going berserk for a while and I felt that the amount of discipline was getting to a troubling level, I might try to slow down the process a little by giving her significantly more instruction. After disciplining her, you might try holding her for a while and letting her calm down. Then, after she has regained her composure you could give her another opportunity to yield. For instance, I might discipline her and then just hold her in my lap for a minute or two saying, "Shhhhh." Then, after she calms down a little, I'd explain it very clearly, "Honey, you don't want another spanking, do you? Good. I don't want to give you another one. But if you do not obey, I will, because that is best for you. I want to help you learn to obey. I want you to say "sorry". Good! Now I'm going to ask you to obey again, and if you do not obey, I'll have to spank again. And you don't want that right? Okay, now, I want you to go and get the toy and give it to me. You must give it to me. You may not set it on the floor. You may not throw it. You may not give it to someone else. You must get the toy and give it to me. Do you understand? Good, now please go and get the toy and hand it to me..."

Give a young child lots of simple instruction. Make it good and clear that you love her and that you will work with her through this issue, but that you will win. You don't want to lose the battle, but you can certainly slow it down a little and give her some time to think through things and make good choices.

With an older child who has a good command of the language, you still need to give plenty of instruction, and it needs to be obeyed. It is important to explain the wisdom behind your instructions at times, but obedience must come first. "Because I said so," is not a bad reason to give. It is important for the child to yield to your authority and not to your ability to develop an air-tight argument persuading your child that your way is best. You can do it a little more politely by saying, "I'll explain it later, but right now I would just like you to do it because I asked you to." Remember that you do not need to convince your child that you are right. Your are the parent; she is the child.

If you are struggling with discipline, give 100% attention to these areas for a few weeks and see if you notice any change. You should not have lots and lots of long, drawn out battles. If your consistent love, discipline, and instruction are not curbing behavior, then I'd keep reevaluating the situation and continuing to get input. Keep praying for wisdom. Ask God to reveal to you anything that you can change to help turn the situation. He wants to help you.

Will Discipline Cause Rebellion?

Some parents shy away from disciplining their children be-cause they are afraid their kids will rebel against the discipline. This is especially true of parents of children who are more prone to push the limits and challenge authority.

I'd be careful not to shy away from disciplining a child because you are not sure how he will respond. Obediently fol-low God in how God has led you to discipline. Then trust Him with the outcome. Most people who believe in spanking seem to recommend it for blatant disobedience. If you do not disci-pline for blatant disobedience, rebellion is sure to flourish. If you inconsistently discipline for disobedience, rebellion is sure to flourish. If you consistently discipline for disobedience, your child will learn that disobedience does not pay, and instead brings unpleasant circumstances. If you are consistent, firm, and loving, this type of discipline will greatly reduce rebellious behavior.

If a parent is not in the habit of setting standards and disciplining his child when those standards are broken, then sure, I'd expect a major flare-up of rebellion. When a cowboy tries to break a wild horse, my movie watching experience tells me that that horse is not going to like it. The horse is going to go absolutely out of control for a time, until it realizes that it is not going to win. Then it eventually calms down and behaves. I'd expect the same thing from a child who is being trained for the first time, or trained consistently for the first time.

Don't waiver on this. If your child wants to challenge your authority, rise to the challenge. It's time to go to battle. That is the loving and right thing to do. God has put you in charge, and expects that you can and will win. Don't fear that addressing your child's rebellion will somehow make him worse. I'd be much more afraid that your child's rebellion will destroy him unless it is confronted, and I'd be quick to confront it and deal with it.

Dr. James Dobson put it this way in his book *The New Strong Willed Child*, "In a moment of rebellion, a little child will consider his parents' wishes and defiantly choose to disobey. Like a military general before a battle, he will calculate the potential risk, marshal his forces, and attack the enemy with guns blazing. When that nose-to-nose confrontation occurs between generations, it is extremely important for the adult to display confidence and decisiveness. The child has made it clear that he's looking for a fight, and his parents would be wise not to disappoint him! Nothing is more destructive to parental leadership than for a mother or father to equivocate [or waffle] during that struggle."

Don't get me wrong, our family has an extremely loving atmosphere. We hang out, hug, tease, and horseplay all the time. However, as parents, we also establish our God-given authority when they are young and we don't let up much as they get older. I'll look my 12-year-old in the eye and say, "Do you want to go to battle? If you want to go to battle I'm up for that, and I'll win, but it'd be much better for you to just yield, here and now." Sometimes he yields, and sometimes we go to battle, but in the end, the rebellion is put down, our child's heart is restored, and peace is brought back into the home.

Have faith that as you follow God you'll find the same blessing, and squelch those fears that somehow you're going to mess up your kid. If you follow God's leading, you will certainly not be worse off for it!

Proverbs 29:17 Discipline your son, and he will give you peace; he will bring delight to your soul.

More on Spanking

Because spanking has fallen out of favor in today's society, many are clamoring to show that the Bible does not really teach it. We've already seen that the Bible does teach it, so I don't want to belabor the point. However, I would like to address a few more of the common arguments against spanking. Because they are generally not very convincing arguments, I am only going to deal with each one briefly in a question and answer format.

1. *I've heard that "spanking" is not a biblical word. Why do you use it?*

Language changes over time. I use the word "spanking" because I believe it is the word in the English language that people can most readily associate with loving discipline.

In a few years, as the term continues to lose favor in our society, it will sound far harsher than it does today. The word "chastise" is an accurate translation, but that word is not used or understood by most people. Some translations use words like "strike" and "beat", but those words definitely carry a connotation of abuse in our society, which is not what the Bible teaches.

A few of the newer translations and paraphrases do use the term "spank", including the New Century Version, Living Bible, New Living Translation, and The Message Bible.

2. The clearest verses on spanking are out of the Old testament. Why should we follow those when we do not follow other Old Testament commands?

There are parts of the Old Testament that we do not have to follow, namely the laws that were specifically intended for the Israelites. It often takes some discernment to know which laws still relate to today and which do not. However, in this case it is pretty obvious. The book of Proverbs is not part of the Levitical law. It is a book of wisdom and common sense. As such, there is not a single verse that cannot be applied to every society in every age. Would there be any reason to selectively throw out the verses on the rod and nothing else? That would be a precarious position to defend.

3. The rod is used frequently in the Bible in a figurative sense. How do we know that in Proverbs it should be interpreted literally?

The Greek word "adelfoó", or "brother", is used 343 times in the New Testament. The vast majority of the times that it is used it is not talking about literal siblings. Even though the word does not usually refer to the sibling relationship, in no way does that mean that James and John were not literal brothers.

The existence of the figurative use of a word implies that there is also a literal use. What is this literal use of the word "brother" It is a male sibling. What is this literal use of the word "rod"? It is physical punishment. To say that since some uses of the term "rod" are figurative that all are figurative would be a blatant error of interpretation.

Proverbs 23:13-14 Do not withhold discipline from a child; if you punish him with the rod, he will not die. Punish him with the rod and save his soul from death.

While I do not like the word choice, this is the verse that is sometimes translated using wording like "beat him with the rod" (KJV) or "strike him with the rod" (NAS). The context is clearly literal. This verse is clearly talking about the loving use of physical discipline to correct and train a child. Let there not be any confusion here; there is no reason to take this verse figuratively.

4. I've heard that spanking and hitting have basically the same definition with the exception of where it takes place on the body.

The argument here is that hitting is abuse, spanking is hitting, therefore spanking is abuse. You'll note that I started off addressing spanking by defining what I meant by it. Spanking in our home has no resemblance to abuse or hitting. As addressed earlier, the intent behind discipline defines it far more accurately than the action itself. Knives and scalpels are similarly defined. What differentiates them is how they are used. One use is to take lives, another is to save lives.

5. *Jesus did not force compliance with the disciples.*

Jesus was not their father. In all likelihood their own parents disciplined them biblically when they were growing up. No one is advocating spanking as a means of discipling adults.

6. *The Bible only mentions spanking a handful of times.*

There are only a handful of uses of the word "covet" in the Bible but it still is significant enough that it made it into the Ten Commandments. You could also argue it from the other angle. Depending on how you count, there are only about a dozen verses in the whole Bible directly related to parenting, and these five verses make up a significant part of what the Bible says on the topic.

These are some of the most common arguments against spanking, but let's evaluate the argument itself. At the risk of being blunt, I'd say that many people who use such arguments are not looking to the Bible to find answers, but are trying to defend a position they already hold. They have preconceived ideas that spanking is harmful and cruel. It is no wonder that they go to such lengths to try to explain away a teaching from the Bible that is so straightforward. Of course, that is a faulty assumption. Mean-spirited and abusive discipline is no part of my experience. When loving and biblical spankings are given to children it is indispensably beneficial to them! There is no need to try to explain it away. God's ways work and bring good into our lives!

FROM OUR HOME

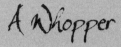

"Did you eat a Whopper®[46]?"

"No," our five-year-old answered, "I did not eat a Whopper®."

Her brother had spotted her, and now she needed to admit it. Kath and I took turns interrogating her (and trying not to laugh).

"Are you sure you did not eat a Whopper®?"

"No, I did not eat a Whopper®," she said adamantly.

"Let me smell your breath."

"Hhhhhhhhaaaaaaaaa."

Her breath smelled suspiciously like chocolate malted milk balls.

"It is important to tell the truth. I can tell you ate a Whopper® because your breath smells like it."

[46] Whopper® is a registered trademark of Hershey

Her eyes vainly searched the room for answers. "No, I did not eat a Whopper® today."

"When did you eat a Whopper®?"

"Daddy gave me some."

"That was yesterday. Did you eat a Whopper® today, because you have some chocolate on your face?"

"No," she said as we watched the gears turn behind her eyes, "I did eat some other chocolate." Her tongue reached out to the corner of her mouth to erase any evidence.

"Show us where you got it."

She took us to the pantry and showed us a bag of piñata candy, which did not contain chocolate.

"Where did you put the wrapper?" Kathleen asked.

"In here," she pointed to the pantry trash.

As Kathleen started digging through the trash our little girl started rethinking where the mystery chocolate wrapper had gone.

"Maybe I put it in the other trash," she reconsidered.

"Okay sweetie, that is enough. You are lying to us." I calmly explained, "I am going to spank you for lying and then I'm going to ask you to tell the truth. If you lie again, I will spank you again until you tell the truth."

We had actually had a similar round of discipline a few weeks before this incident, so I didn't expect this one to go long. Hopefully she learned that she would not win this battle.

I took her to the bathroom and gave her a good long controlled spank. Snatching a Whopper® is not that big of a deal, but telling a whopper is. After I finished I stood her up and gave her a hug.

"Okay honey, tell me the truth now."

"I did *not* eat a Whopper®." (She's got some spunk to her)

"I have to spank you again for lying." Round 2 commenced. As soon as I finished and stood her up, she broke.

"I *did* eat a Whopper®." This time her cries were not from the pain, but from the relief of getting the lie off her chest. I hugged her again.

"Thank you for telling the truth. If you had told the truth in the first place you would have saved yourself a lot of trouble, and from telling more lies. That's the way lies grow. When you tell one, you end up telling more. If you tell a lie, get it right at once so that it does not grow. I love you honey. Now go apologize to your mommy and your brother..."

Proverbs 12:22 The LORD detests lying lips, but he delights in men who are truthful.

– 6 –

Teaching and Training

> *"For precept must be upon precept,*
> *precept upon precept;*
> *line upon line, line upon line;*
> *here a little, and there a little"*
> *— Isaiah 28:10 (KJV)*

The Incubator

Deuteronomy 11:18,19 Fix these words of mine in your hearts and minds; tie them as symbols on your hands and bind them on your foreheads. Teach them to your children, talking about them when you sit at home and when you walk along the road, when you lie down and when you get up.

Imagine a home where the parents yell at the children constantly. They call them names and tell them that they will never amount to anything. The children watch T.V. for hours on end and don't receive any educational or religious training. Pornography, alcohol, and marijuana are available to all of the children from the time that they can walk. The parents leave the children home alone for days on end and never tell them where they are going or when they will be back.

Do you think that would have an impact on those children? Undoubtedly. Yet on the other end of the spectrum, many parents question whether or not bringing a child up in a healthy Christian home will really make a significant difference. If one environment has the potential of utterly destroying a child's future, then shouldn't the opposite environment have the potential of equipping our children as spiritual champions?

Our home is an incubator. It is the best place for our children. Here they are safe from pornography, drugs, and alcohol. We protect them from unrestricted internet and T.V. Everything we read, watch and listen to is filtered. We protect them from lingerie catalogs, "swimsuit issues," and similar unwanted influences. In our home our kids are also safe from ideas that oppose God. Here they can be trained spiritually, emotionally, and intellectually. We can inoculate them to much of what the world has to offer. Our family provides a safe and loving atmosphere where girls will become women, and boys will become men.

Our goal is not to keep them from the world forever. We are not trying to withdraw from the world, but to reach out to it. We want our kids to be world-changers. But for now they are in our incubator—growing, learning, maturing.

There are countless things we want to train our kids in, ranging from not standing up in the highchair to sharing their faith with their friends at school. The following articles will address several different areas of training, or ways of thinking about training that have been helpful to us.

The Invisible Parent (The Power of Instruction)

Have you ever wished that when your children go off to school or college someday that you could go with them and coach them? Wouldn't it be great if you could be right there with them as they go through their days, gently watching over them, giving them advice, and guiding them? I know that sounds pretty intrusive, but maybe you could turn invisible and just whisper in their ears now and then. If you could somehow remove the obnoxious part of it, wouldn't you want the instructive part of it?

That is exactly the role that your teachings should take in your children's lives:

> *Proverbs 6:20-23 My son, keep your father's commands and do not forsake your mother's teaching. Bind them upon your heart forever; fasten them around your neck. When you walk, they will guide*

you; when you sleep, they will watch over you; when you awake, they will speak to you. For these commands are a lamp, this teaching is a light, and the corrections of discipline are the way to life.

Did you catch that? If our kids lock into our teachings and hold them close to their hearts, those bits of instruction will guide them when they walk, watch over them when they sleep, and speak to them when they are awake. What we teach our kids will light their ways through life, and the times we've corrected them will bring them the good life.

The instruction we give our kids will profoundly impact their lives if it is godly teaching and if we can get them to grasp hold of it. The godly teaching part of it is pretty simple. Pass on to them everything written in Proverbs. It is a guide to godly living. It was inspired by God and written by the wisest man who has ever lived, so that is a great place to start.

How do you get them to grab hold of it? First, we must give attention to living out what we are trying to impart to our children. It is crucial that we are the pacesetters in life, because *much is caught, not taught.*

Second, we must give our kids a great deal of teaching. Studies show that we only remember 10% of what we hear. Given that piece of information, you may want to start by teaching your kids ten times as much. Repeat simple truths that you want to ingrain in them again, and again, and again.

- You reap what you sow. (Galatians 6:7)
- Do to others what you would have them do to you. (Matthew 7:12)
- Use only speech that builds. (Ephesians 4:29)
- Work with all your heart. (Colossians 3:23)
- God always sees. (Job 34:21)

If you ingrain simple truths like these into your children and you maintain a loving and corrective atmosphere in your home, these teachings will continue to ring through their ears, and guide them for their entire lives.

With that hope and promise, we build into the lives of our children.

Making Training Effective — Keeping Them in the Barrel

Proverbs 15:10 Stern discipline awaits him who leaves the path; he who hates correction will die.

Do you know the difference between a pistol and a rifle? I don't know much about guns, but I know that one of the reasons a rifle is more accurate is because the barrel is longer and therefore keeps the bullet on a straight path longer. By the time it leaves the tip of the gun it has already been on its path for some time. If the barrel were only two inches long, or if there were no barrel at all, the bullet would be far more likely to stray off path.

Imagine a superball being thrown through a culvert or a large metal pipe. When it came out the other end, its path would have been affected by the environment it passed through. Now, imagine shooting it through a tube of wrapping paper. The ball's bouncing would be even more constricted, and so when it left the tube it would fly straighter. Now imagine throwing it through a tube that was just slightly larger than the ball. You'd have to shoot it like a blow-dart. How would that affect the flight of the ball? That's exactly what the barrel of a gun does. It constricts the path of the bullet for a time so that when it leaves the barrel it flies straight.

Parenting is like shooting a gun. The longer and the more constraining the barrel is, the straighter the bullet flies. The longer children are trained, and the more disciplined their training is, the more likely it is that they will head down a path consistent with their training when they leave the home. Of course, just like a gun barrel, you don't want to constrain them so much that the gun barrel explodes. You don't want them to become exasperated and give up hope.

> *You need to constrain their path—not too much, and not too little.*

That's one of the keys to training kids. You need to constrain their path—not too much, and not too little. And you want to do it for a long time, developing a pattern of following the right path in their life. If you keep a tight path for them to travel down, you can expect them to not stray too far from the path.

But thanks be to God, though you used to be slaves to sin, you have come to obey from your heart the pattern of teaching that has now claimed your allegiance. Romans 6:17 (TNIV)

Though we used to be slaves to sin, we've learned to obey. Is it simply a dutiful obedience? No, it is from our heart. How was it developed? It was developed by following a pattern of teaching. At first that following may have been just out of duty, but now it has claimed our allegiance and we obey from the heart.

This is the same principle. If you set a pattern, a track, a path for your children, it will guide their flight through life.

Proverbs 22:6 Train a child in the way he should go, and when he is old he will not turn from it.

Teaching Them to Sit and Play Quietly

A tip we've learned from others in our church is blanket time. Blanket time is when we ask our younger children to sit and play quietly on a blanket. Blanket time is not a discipline tool, but it is a training tool. In other words, we don't use it after they get into trouble as a time-out, but we use it whenever we want a few minutes of structure or we want our kids to have some set boundaries.

The principle is pretty simple. You just put your kids on a blanket and tell them they may not get off until you say so. Set whatever other boundaries you want for the time. You can give them toys if you want, let them watch a video, or give them books. For us, blanket time usually means quiet time.

Tell the child that if she gets off or fusses she will get spanked. This will train her to be able to play quietly and to play within boundaries. Believe it or not, this will often calm a restless child. Kids need and crave boundaries.

After the initial training period your child should get accustomed to this pretty quickly and will be able to sit and play quietly for 30 minutes to an hour.

Here's the beauty of it: now you can go to any meeting anywhere, pull out your blanket and have your kids play quietly while you talk to a friend, attend a class at church, or sign mortgage papers. It's awesome, and it's incredibly freeing for both the parent *and* the child!

Quickly, Completely, and Cheerfully

We ask our kids to obey quickly, completely, and cheerfully. It is important to understand that discipline is not just about getting the right actions, but it is also about getting the right actions with the right heart. A child who is responding with a good heart will respond correctly in these three areas.

1. Quickly.

When I ask my kids to do something I'd like them to get right on it. If they are in the middle of doing something else (which they usually are), then it is okay if they ask if they can finish what they are doing first. However, if I say, "No", as I often do, I'd like them to drop their playing or Nintendo® game and do what I asked. Doing so demonstrates an ability to obey even when it conflicts with their interests. They need to understand that they are under the authority of their parents, and we have the right to manage their time.

2. Completely.

When we give them a job to do, they need to do it all the way. If we ask them to do something, and they do something else first, then they did not obey completely. If we ask them not to eat any candy, and they eat just one piece, then they are not obeying completely.

3. Cheerfully.

While it is better to obey begrudgingly than it is to not obey at all, it is still not ideal. We strive to have our kids respond cheerfully when it comes to their nonverbal behavior and voice tone.

Teaching the Bible Stories

1 Corinthians 10:11 These things happened to them as examples and were written down as warnings for us, on whom the fulfillment of the ages has come.

A few months before our son Blaise turned four, he asked us about a man who had just moved away. The man had made a set of bad decisions in his life, culminating in him fleeing town. Blaise questioned, "Is he running from God just like Jonah did?" I was a little shocked and had to think about it for a second and then I replied, "Yeah, that is exactly what he is doing!"

That's pretty profound for a three-year-old! Our goal is to have our children know and apply Bible stories to their lives like that. Jonah is not the only story in the Bible that has real life application. 1 Corinthians 10 talks about many of the events that happened to Israel and says they were written down for us as examples that we should learn from. All the stories in the Bible contain incredible gems of truth about who God is and how He relates to mankind.

We've always been impressed with how quickly kids learn. Our kids will watch a video once and start quoting the lines. Sometimes they will even start to quote lines from videos that they haven't even seen, but have only heard described to them by their friends. By the time they watch a video three times, they've got it down amazingly well. It didn't take long for us to question if we could use this to our advantage.

When Blaise was little, I got a bonus at work and we put much of it toward buying Christian videos. We set our boy in front of the T.V. and let him soak it in. He watched them again and again and again. Sure enough, it had a profound impact on him. We even suspect that Psalty the singing songbook is the one who led him to the Lord! Since that time we've included videos and DVDs as a part of nearly every Christmas and birthday and have developed quite a collection. What an incredibly easy way to pass biblical truth on to children!

Of course, I wouldn't overdo the video thing. I can't leave all the spiritual development of my children to Veggie Tales®. Videos are powerful and simple tools, but there are countless other ideas. You can also tell the stories yourself using dramatic gestures and funny voices. As kids get older, you can have them tell the stories to you, or even have them act out the stories. Have older kids read stories to younger kids. Other resources include children's story Bibles, the Bible on tape, and audio tapes that have Bible stories. On some days you may have a theme: Have them read the book of Jonah out of the Bible, watch a video on Jonah, and then quiz them on the book of Jonah before bed.

The Bible is an exciting book, full of life-changing stories. Your kids will love learning it. Do you, the parent, value them learning the Bible enough to prioritize it over other "entertainment"? That is the real question!

Teaching with Intent

Our church recently started a 16-week plan to read through the New Testament together. I was shocked when a college student said, "I've been going to church for almost my whole life and I've never read through the New Testament." That's heart breaking! The New Testament is not very big. It's roughly two thirds the size of most novels. Even though our faith is founded upon it, many people have never read the whole thing. Some people have been following Christ for twenty or thirty years and have yet to read through the New Testament. If you haven't done so yet, please do so. It's such a small thing to do.

How much effort would it take to get your child to read through the New Testament? There are 260 chapters in the New Testament. If he read one chapter a day it would take 8 ½ months. Two chapters a day would take four months and a week. Three chapters a day would take 12 ½ weeks.

You'd have to have your kid sit down and read for a little while each day. That would take some time on your part, but not much. The reading would have both spiritual and educational benefits. Since it is good for us all, maybe you could even do it with him. It would provide some great parent time, as well as setting a good example.

Little things like this over a lifetime will profoundly impact your children. They don't take much time, but they make a real difference in their lives. Sometimes we view stuff like this as being so difficult that we don't even try a little.

I read a book called *Ten P's in a Pod* by Arnold Pent III. It's about a couple and their eight children who drove all over the country preaching the benefits of Bible-reading. One of the philosophies of their father was that you should feed your soul more than you feed your body. As a result, he had family devotions for 30 minutes after each meal. This was in addition to their private devotions which were 30 minutes for the younger kids and 60 minutes for the older ones. The book claims that the kids were of normal intelligence and had normal memories. Yet the amazing thing is that without really focusing intensively on memorization, the kids could quote massive amounts of Scripture from memory. They just read the Bible that much! One of the older children could quote the entire New Testament almost entirely from memory. I was impressed!

I'm not saying all of you should do that with your kids. What I'm saying is that we can get fooled into thinking that doing stuff like having our kids read through the New Testament is really excellent parenting—almost extreme. Having your kids memorize the New Testament is extreme parenting. Having them read through the New Testament is far closer to mediocre parenting.

Perhaps the thought of achieving excellence can be so overwhelming that we can lose heart and even give up trying for mediocrity. It would do us well to raise the bar a little in our expectations. Of course, the hardest part of this is that such parenting can conflict with other things we are trying to accomplish. Let me ask you a question. How much are you willing to do to win with your kids? Are you willing to read the Bible yourself? Will you pray for fifteen minutes a day? Are you willing to get more involved at church? We need to be strong and be willing to do whatever it takes.

1 Corinthians 16:13 Be on your guard; stand firm in the faith; be men of courage; be strong.

The School of Hard Knocks

Romans 5:3-4 Not only so, but we also rejoice in our sufferings, because we know that suffering produces perseverance; perseverance, character; and character, hope.

Note the progression in this verse: suffering→perseverance →character→hope.

There is much hope in life as we grow in character. That character is produced through suffering as we go through trials. Character can't be taught through book learning; it is developed as we respond to the pressures we face.

You'll find that great men and women of God typically have a history of hardship. Their suffering is not inconsequential to who they have become. On the contrary, their trials are paramount to their godly development.

The story of Joseph in Genesis 30-50 is a great example of this. At the beginning of the story he seems like an arrogant brat; by the end of the story he is a world leader. What happened in the middle? He was thrown into a pit, betrayed by his brothers, sold into slavery, tossed into jail, and forgotten by the cupbearer. His father's pampering didn't do much for him in the early years, but later on, the trials he faced chiseled him into a man of God.

Examples abound. Great men and women of God have lives full of hardship. Consider Abram, Sarai, Hannah, David, Elizabeth, and Peter. All of them faced great suffering in their lives. This certainly was not without effect in their character development.

"It is doubtful that God can use a man greatly until He has hurt him deeply."

—A.W. Tozer

"It is doubtful that God can use a man greatly until He has hurt him deeply."

—A.W. Tozer

One of our goals as parents is to help our kids develop character. A way to accomplish this is to introduce trials into their lives. I'm not implying that we should be cruel to our children. I'm saying that we should make their lives challenging. Here are three practical ways to shape our kids' character through making their lives challenging.

School – Regardless of how you choose to educate your children, I would encourage you to push them to excel. I can't tell you the number of times I've thought one of our kids was learning something that was less than valuable. No offense to our northern neighbors, but I don't care if my kids learn the Canadian providences and capitals. I don't care if they can identify 100 species of flowers, or if they can name the inventor of the cotton gin. However, I care greatly that they learn to apply themselves and study diligently, especially when doing so is difficult. School is a trial in their lives, and responding correctly to it will help shape their character. Encourage your kids to excel in school. It will help them in countless ways in life.

We do not hesitate to help the kids do well at school by giving extra school work or by setting high academic standards. If a child does poorly on a test because he was not diligent and did not study, there are consequences. We figure out a way to make him learn the material. We might have him retake the test for us, write out everything he missed twenty times, or write out and study note cards for the whole chapter. We see an educational benefit to this, but more importantly, we view it as a healthy part of the development of their moral fiber.

Sports – We don't have our kids involved in a lot of sports because we don't have the time to run them all over town. We started our oldest in soccer and saw how much time it took. We then multiplied that time commitment by the number of kids we had at the time and decided that wasn't going to work well for us. However, sports can be another great way to teach kids to persevere through trials. When you push your body to do what it does not want to do, it gives you a confidence that you can force your flesh to obey your mind. If our kids are going to do sports they need to work hard at them. They need to discipline their minds and train their bodies. I do not care if they are athletic, but I do care that they develop character in whatever they are involved in.

Chores – As kids grow older they can help around the house a lot. They can do dishes, laundry, mowing, raking, vacuuming, sweeping, mopping, and just about anything that needs to be done. Obviously, you need to be a hard worker yourself and set a good example, but there is no need for you to be slaving away while your seven-year-old watches T.V. or plays Nintendo®. Most kids get far too much entertainment. They need to learn how to work and how to work hard.

Directing Personal Choices

Proverbs 22:15 Young people are prone to foolish-ness and fads; the cure comes through tough-minded discipline. (The Message)

Many parents question whether or not they should inter-fere with their children's personal choices. Should you let your kids pierce their ears, noses, navels, or tongues? Is it okay if they stay out late, or even all night? Can they cut off all their hair, grow it long, make it spiked, or dye it orange? Is it all right if they wear mini-skirts, tube tops, a dog collar, or dress com-pletely in black? Is it okay if they get tattooed? Should you let them smoke if they want to? Can they pick their own friends?

These questions relate to personal choices. However, that fact does not limit your authority and responsibility to set boundaries. God, in His infinite wisdom, has given *your* chil-dren to *you* to parent. He wants *you* to use *your* wisdom to lovingly guide and direct *them.*

Almost all choices could be viewed as personal, and almost all choices have social impacts. Education affects a child's personhood. It is your responsibility to guide and direct the educational process. It would be wrong to just say, "Who am I to force my child to be educated? Is that really my right?" That's ridiculous. As parents we jump in and encourage our kids to study and to learn as much as they can because we believe that will help them develop certain life skills and help equip them for adulthood.

If we can direct choices such as education, then we should see that other more personal life choices can and should also be directed, because they also affect a child's ability to succeed and be a positive contributor to society.

Their habits, dress, appearance, and even friends affect everything about your children: social circles, employment opportunities, ability to relate to others, and effectiveness in outreach. This being the case, it only makes sense to interfere in their lives and direct them in ways that would be good for them.

Parents can often be fooled into thinking that choices in such areas are important for kids to make on their own because that is their identity. I don't believe this is the case. You, as the parent, are shaping their identity in many ways. Instead of focusing on our child's personality and preferences, we should focus on who the Bible says they are and their identity in Christ. Typically, what teens are expressing in these areas is not their identity, but their rebellion against the standards of their home and society. If so gifted, your children can be artsy,

> Having them cut their hair, cover up their bodies, and look basically human is not some kind of horrible dogmatic repression.

creative people without rebelling against society. Having them cut their hair, cover up their bodies, and look basically human is not some kind of horrible dogmatic repression. Instead, it is the loving, guiding hand of parents who clearly understand their God-given authority in their children's lives.

Religion Crammed Down the Throat (Teaching Religion)

Deuteronomy 6:6-9 These commandments that I give you today are to be upon your hearts. Impress them on your children. Talk about them when you sit at home and when you walk along the road, when you lie down and when you get up. Tie them as symbols on your hands and bind them on your foreheads. Write them on the doorframes of your houses and on your gates.

Do you ever fear that your children will rebel against God because you made them go to youth group, church, or AWANA? We all know people who say that they had religion crammed down their throats when they were younger. Please take a moment and reread the above verse. What does it say? How much religion should we expose our children to—a little, or a lot? To me it sounds like it is far more than a lot. We are supposed to totally engulf them in God's Word. Our home should be an environment where God is talked about when we get up, when we eat meals, when we go for walks, and when we lie down. In other words, the things of God should be a constant topic of conversation.

Stop and think about it for a second. How many of the people you've heard say that religion was crammed down their throats actually had religion crammed down their throats?

Some of the people I know are just bitter that they had to attend lifeless and rote services. Others may have been turned off by extensive hypocrisy they saw in the church they attended. Hopefully that is not what we are exposing our children to. If we are, we need to stop! That was the type of meaningless religion Jesus opposed.

Others who say religion was crammed down their throats may just be blaming God for their own rebellion against Him. It's like when someone gets caught speeding and they blame the "stupid law" or the "cops who don't have anything better to do." The real problem is not with the law or the police; the problem is with the lawbreaker. In the same way, when someone is rebelling against God it may be easier to blame their upbringing rather than admitting they have an issue with God.

Don't worry about giving them too much; worry about if you are giving them enough.

Are there really people out there who were exposed to good teaching in a healthy church, a loving family, and surrounded by godly Christians who are still resentful of their upbringing? My guess would be that it would be a pretty small group, if any at all. Even though they might be resentful of their upbringing, they would still be profoundly impacted by it for the better.

The real issue here is not typically over involvement in church; it's usually hypocrisy in our own lives that leaves a bad taste in the mouths of kids. It is sobering to think that our own Christian example as parents could be the very thing that makes our kids bitter toward God.

Is it better to over-educate or under-educate a student? Is

it better to over-train or under-train a soldier? Is it better to over-expose or under-expose our kids to God? In each of these cases, more is better! Greater exposure to the things of God should only result in a greater love toward God, and should better equip your kids for life. Don't worry that you might push them away from God! Worry about how you are going to make them excited about God. Don't worry about giving them too much; worry about if you are giving them enough.

Negative Training (Bad Influences)

What do you do if your kids are associating with "bad" kids? I'm not talking about the type that light cats on fire, but just kids that are a little ornery, rambunctious, or are bad influences. Should you separate your children from the children who are negative influences, or should you hope that your own children can positively influence the others?

We've been in different small groups at times when the ice breaker was, "Who was the worst influence on you as a kid?" The most common answer has always been 'neighbors.' I suppose if we were to think of the worst things we've ever done in our lives, most of them were done with someone else—a neighbor or a close friend. Having a friend there gave us a chance to prove how cool we were or to receive approval for our acts of deviousness. In looking back at our own childhoods, we can see that it would be wise to not underestimate the influence of friends.

The Bible says it straight out, "Do not be misled: 'Bad company corrupts good character'" (1 Corinthians 15:33). If your child hangs out too much with bad influences, there is a good chance that he will be *influenced* for the *bad*. Your child can be corrupted by friends, just like the metal on your car can be corrupted when exposed to water.

Your child certainly can influence others for the good and should do so as his character is developed. We haven't hit the teen years yet, but I wouldn't expect younger kids to withstand significant amounts of peer pressure, because their character is not well formed. It is still being actively developed. While it's possible for the good kid to lead the bad kid, what's possible may not be as important at the moment as taking a look at what is happening. Is your child influencing the bad influence, or is your child being negatively influenced? With some kids our kids will lead out; with others they tend to resort to becoming followers. We tell them, "If you can't lead, then follow someone who is making good choices."

If our child was being negatively influenced we would:

1) Limit the amount of time he is exposed to the bad influence.
2) Closely monitor the children's activities and speech when they are together.
3) Withdraw my child from the situation if it became severe enough.

For example, if our child was around a negative influence at a weekly playdate, I might shorten the playdate from three to one-and-a-half hours. I'd also try to supervise the situation more closely. If I still felt that my child was being negatively impacted, I might quit going to the playdate altogether.

What if the child is not bad, but just ornery or rambunctious? You are the only one who can accurately assess the impact on your child. However, if it gets bad enough that you're asking the question, my guess is that it is bad enough that you'll want to do something about it. You obviously don't want the behavior that you've seen imitated by your child. So, in light of that, I'd put some sort of boundaries on the relationship.

That said, I want my kids to be in the world and influencing the world. But I don't want them in over their heads. They need to be mature enough to handle it.

FROM OUR HOME

Moonstruck

Psalms 136:3-9 Give thanks to the Lord of Lords...who made the great lights...the sun to govern the day... the moon and stars to govern the night; His love endures forever.

"Moon daddy! Mooooon!" my two-year-old exclaimed from the back of the car.

"Yeah buddy, the moon.," I disinterestedly acknowledged for the fourteen billionth time.

He pleaded, "Mooo-oo-oo-oon!" hoping for a more excited response.

My first son's excitement over the moon was quite extreme. Often the first words from his mouth after a night's sleep were, "Where did moon go daddy?" And off we went to check the skies.

I must admit that his excitement over the moon started to rub off on me. I had never really thought much about the moon before. I would catch myself looking for it and mentally noting when I saw it, where it was in relation to the day before, and what phase it was in. I also enjoyed trying to explain this to my son who described its movement as, "Moon go up, up, up, up, down, down, down, down. See no more."

The moon is such a majestic display of God's artistic creativity. What a simple and yet awesome display of his power and greatness. All of creation proclaims God's majesty. It leaves a trail of evidence pointing to a great mastermind Creator who is infinite in ability and love.

I always wondered how I was going to explain the concept of God to my children, but it was much easier than I imagined. I simply said, "Yeah! That's the moon! Isn't it neat? Did you know that God made that for us? He must really love us, huh?"

Satisfied for a moment, my son would contemplate this, and the many other wonders God gave him to explore.

Training for Life's Temptations

Proverbs 22:6 Train a child in the way he should go, and when he is old he will not turn from it.

What does it mean to "train" a child? Training involves many different elements but the big picture is that we are equipping them to handle upcoming challenges in their lives. A coach trains an athlete for competition and we train our kids for life. We had a young lady in our church that was training a guide dog. A major part of that training was to try to teach the dog to act predictably in unpredictable situations. You can't just train the dog how to walk beside you and obey certain commands, but the dog also needs to respond well when a child comes up to pet it, when it sees another dog, or when a squirrel runs in front of it. These are unpredictable but expected situations.

In training our kids we need to think about the obvious things like education, work ethic, and manners, but we also need to think about training them for inevitable temptations.

What should your son do when the clerk bends over and her blouse falls open?

What should your daughter do when a car full of guys whistles at her?

How do you want your kids to respond when someone tries to introduce them to alcohol or drugs?

Think through your own life. What have been your greatest challenges or temptations? What mistakes have you seen others make? How can you help train your own kids to make the best choices in these situations? If you train them in these things it will help them stay on a good course in life.

We know a pastor named Mark Darling who used newspaper articles as one method of training his children. When two kids are playing with a gun and one shoots his friend accidentally, use that as an opportunity to talk to your kids about guns. When a stranger abducts a child, use that as a warning to not talk to strangers. A sample discussion might go something like this:

"Hey kids! Come here. Do you see this picture? It's of a car that wrecked and wrapped right around that telephone pole. A boy was driving 100 MPH and he got killed. He killed his three best friends too. Some day when you're old enough to drive it'll be tempting to go fast. It's fun to go fast, isn't it? I bet they were having a lot of fun before the car went out of control. But we have laws to protect us. They are for our own good. This boy didn't mean to hurt anyone; he was just having fun. Now four kids are dead. All their families are sad and all their friends are sad. It's terrible isn't it? I want you to remember to always drive carefully because I love you and I don't ever want you to get hurt. And I don't want you to hurt anyone else either."

Then we'd let them ask questions and talk through it some

more. The goal isn't to unnecessarily scare them. It's to necessarily scare them, and to help them learn from the mistakes of others. God does this all the time in the Bible. He tells people to do something, and then He tells them all the bad consequences they will face if they do not listen. He is trying to drive points home, and we need to do the same.

> *The goal isn't to unnecessarily scare them. It's to necessarily scare them, and to help them learn from the mistakes of others.*

The Greatest Teacher (The Stranger)

Author unknown

A few months before I was born, my dad met a stranger who was new to our small Tennessee town. From the beginning, Dad was fascinated with this enchanting newcomer, and soon invited him to live with our family. The stranger was quickly accepted and was around to welcome me into the world a few months later.

As I grew up, I never questioned his place in our family. In my young mind, each member had a special niche. My brother, Bill, five years my senior, was my example. Fran, my younger sister, gave me an opportunity to play 'big brother' and develop the art of teasing. My parents were complementary instructors—Mom taught me to love the Word of God, and Dad taught me to obey it.

But the stranger was our storyteller. He could weave the most fascinating tales. Adventures, mysteries, and comedies were daily conversations. He could hold our whole family spell-bound for hours each evening. If I wanted to know about politics, history, or science, he knew it all. He knew about the past, understood the present, and seemingly could predict the future. The pictures he could draw were so lifelike that I would often laugh or cry as I watched. He was like a friend to the whole family. The stranger was our storyteller.

He took Dad, Bill, and me to our first major league baseball game. He was always encouraging us to see the movies, and he even made arrangements to introduce us to several movie stars. My brother and I were deeply impressed by John Wayne in particular.

The stranger was an incessant talker. Dad didn't seem to mind, but sometimes Mom would quietly get up—while the rest of us were enthralled with one of his stories of faraway places—go to her room, read her Bible and pray. I wonder now if she ever prayed that the stranger would leave.

You see, my dad ruled our household with certain moral convictions. But this stranger never felt an obligation to honor them. Profanity, for example, was not allowed in our house—not from us, from our friends, or adults. Our longtime visitor, however, used occasional four-letter words that burned my ears and made Dad squirm. To my knowledge the stranger was never confronted.

My dad was a teetotaler who didn't permit alcohol in his home—not even for cooking. But the stranger felt like we needed exposure and enlightened us to other ways of life. He offered us beer and other alcoholic beverages often. He made cigarettes look tasty, cigars manly, and pipes distinguished.

He talked freely (probably too much and too freely) about sex. His comments were sometimes blatant, sometimes suggestive, and generally embarrassing. I know now that my early concepts of the man-woman relationship were influenced by the stranger. As I look back, I believe it was by the grace of God that the stranger did not influence us more. Time after time he opposed the values of my parents. Yet he was seldom rebuked and never asked to leave.

More than thirty years have passed since the stranger moved in with the young family on Morningside Drive. He is not nearly so intriguing to my dad as he was in those early years. But if I were to walk into my parents' den today, you would still see him sitting over in a corner, waiting for someone to listen to him talk and watch him draw his pictures.

His name? We always just called him T.V.

Teaching for Their Good

A man walks into a store that sells sporting goods and says that he wants to purchase everything that he will need for a seven-day back country backpacking trip. The clerk gathers up a backpack, cooking supplies, a tent, prepackaged foods, a rope, hiking boots, and other miscellaneous supplies. While he works his way through the store, the two talk and it becomes obvious to the clerk that the man he is helping has never camped a day in his life. As the man finishes paying and turns to leave the store the clerk says, "Good luck! Have a great time!"

A second man walks into a second store and asks the clerk for exactly the same things. When the clerk becomes aware that the camper is inexperienced he starts offering advice. He discusses with the customer how to avoid contact with bears, how to keep from getting lost, and what to do in the case of a sudden storm. The clerk encourages him not to go alone, where to camp, and not to drink the water out of the streams. He picks out a first aid kit for him and talks briefly about snake bites, altitude sickness, and hypothermia. As he turns to leave the clerk says, "One more thing, make sure you tell someone where you are going and when you'll be back."

When the first guy leaves the store he thinks, "Man that guy was really helpful!" and he heads off on his trip.

The second guy leaves the store and thinks, "Man that guy was obnoxious! Did he think I was an idiot? I can't believe he was harping on me like that. I couldn't wait to get out of there."

Which camper do you think had the better time? Even though the second clerk's instructions may have been a little overbearing, they were needed. The first camper was far more likely to end up raided by bears, lost, or dehydrated.

We need to remember that. Even though our kids are not always overly appreciative about the guidance we give them, it is desperately needed.

Look at how God instructs Israel:

Deuteronomy 10:12-13 And now, O Israel, what does the LORD your God ask of you but to fear the LORD your God, to walk in all His ways, to love Him, to serve the LORD your God with all your heart and with all your soul, and to observe the LORD's commands and decrees that I am giving you today for your own good?

Notice how clearly the Bible lays out exactly what they need to know:

* Fear the LORD
* Walk in His ways
* Love Him
* Serve Him wholeheartedly
* Observe His commands

And then what does He do? He says that these instructions are "for your own good."

Being human, I'm sure the Israelites weren't terribly fond of being told what to do, but God told them anyway, because it was for their own good.

We need to remember this with our children. While they may, at times, be resentful of our boundaries and instructions, we are giving them for their own good. In the end they will respect us for it and see that we had their best interests in mind. Don't worry about being too strict; worry about protecting your children through your guidance.

Missionaries or Mission Fields

In our group of churches there is a saying that your children will either be missionaries or mission fields. I don't know who said it first, but it's a powerful concept. Your children will be actively trying to reach someone else, or someone else will be trying to reach your children. They will be proclaiming the word of Christ, or they will be having some other teaching proclaimed to them. They will be visionary or will be open to someone else's vision.

That's a scary thought! I actually talked to a young missionary once who belonged to a group that I would consider a cult. He had been involved in a Christian church in his youth, so I asked him how he got involved in his new church. He said that when he was a teenager some missionaries came by the house and preached to him and convinced him of the teachings of his new religion. What a graphic picture of this concept! How his parents must have regretted not equipping him to face such false teachings!

So how can you equip your kids to be "missionaries?" Here are a few practical ideas:

1) Have them memorize some basic gospel verses. (We start with the following ten passages: 1 John 5:13; John 3:16; Romans 3:23; Romans 6:23; James 2:10; Ephesians 2:8,9; Romans 5:8; John 3:36; John 14:6; John 5:24)

2) Have your kids pray daily for their friends and neighbors who have not yet believed in Christ. This will help them develop a heart for those who are lost.

3) Teach your kids an outreach program like the Romans Road, How to Share Your Faith Without an Argument, the Four Spiritual Laws, or the bridge diagram.

4) Get Christian biographies for your kids to read. The *Trailblazers* series is great at telling the stories in a readable fashion. (Not all books in this series are appropriate for all ages.) This will help your kids see Christianity lived out at its fullest as it looks from several different vantage points.

5) Be actively involved in a church where a faith-filled Christian life is lived out and demonstrated by a majority of the members. You and your spouse are only two parts of the body of Christ. Your child needs to see people expressing a whole variety of gifts that the two of you may not demonstrate strongly.

6) Model it! Devote your own life to wholeheartedly living for Christ and to spreading His message of forgiveness to all who believe.

7) Have your kids develop a habit of reading their Bibles daily. (Of course you'll need to model this for them.)

8) As your kids get older, have them read faith building books like *More than a Carpenter* (Josh McDowell), *Evidence that Demands a Verdict* (Josh McDowell), and *Five Crucial Questions about Christianity* (Tom Short).

9) Talk often with your kids about their purpose in life. If they do not have a strong, clear purpose to live for, they could give their life to anything and anyone.

10) Kids are followers or leaders. While we would like all of our kids to be leaders, some are not naturally bent that way. We would be reluctant to let a "follower" be overly influenced by peers until we are confident that our child could lead out with a gospel mindset. Don't release your kids too soon! In other words, do not give them more responsibility and independence than they are equipped to handle.

Of course, it is hard to give a definitive ten point all-inclusive program. Those are just a few starter ideas. The reality is that we all need to seek God's guidance and wisdom with each of our kids. I would not assume that passing on our faith or heart for God is going to be an automatic slam dunk. Being evangelistic (or even just *different*) is not easy for most of us. This will be a fierce battle for our kids, especially when they hit the teen years, which is when kids are so easily obsessed with what others think of them. Pray for wisdom. This is no easy task.

Training to Love

Matthew 22:36-40 "Teacher, which is the greatest commandment in the Law?"

Jesus replied: "'Love the Lord your God with all your heart and with all your soul and with all your mind.' This is the first and greatest commandment. And the second is like it: 'Love your neighbor as yourself.' All the Law and the Prophets hang on these two commandments."

Can you imagine a flight instructor who teaches his students everything about airplanes but never teaches them how to fly? This oversight would be analogous to a Christian parent failing to teach his children how to love. Love is not just an extra in the life of a Christian; it is central to our purpose and calling.

I receive many questions that could be answered by the above verse: "Is it okay for children to be squabbling all the time?" "My six-year-old says he doesn't like me. Is that okay?" "My older child doesn't want his little sister hanging around when his friend is over. Is it okay for him to tell her to go away?"

If we get all caught up in how important it is for children to act like kids, express their feelings, and be treated like their peers, then these questions can be difficult. However, if we keep in mind that the most important thing we are passing on to our children is love, and that they need to become experts at love to live the life God has called them to, then the answers should be clear. Your kids shouldn't bicker and be getting on each other's nerves all the time because that would not be

Love is not just an extra in the life of a Christian; it is central to our purpose and calling.

loving. Regardless of how they feel, they shouldn't say, "I don't like you," to anyone, because that is not loving. They shouldn't exclude others from their play because that is not loving.

I'm not saying that there is never an exception to these behaviors, but we need to train for the rule, not just for the exceptions to the rule. For example, you should train your kids to include younger kids in their play at home, church, or school. You can occasionally give them time just with their peers, but train them to love. Is there a balance? Is there an exception? Fine, then teach that. Teach your kids how to say they are upset at you without using hateful words or tones. Help them learn how to work through conflict without constant arguing. Teach them how to love in difficult situations.

Do any of these statements ring a bell? Turn the other cheek. Anyone who wants to be great must be a servant. Wash one another's feet. Do to others what you would have them do to you. Forgive 70 times 7 times. Give to the needy. Do not judge. As I have loved you, so you must love one another...

Each of these phrases could be expanded upon with a book of its own, but you are familiar with the sayings. They are things that Jesus taught. His teachings were saturated with instructions on how to love people.

By all means, don't let hurtful words or actions go unchecked in your home. Jesus viewed love as the most important command. It should also be the most important thing that you pass on to your kids and the most important code of conduct for their behavior.

- 7 -
Conclusion

The state of the Christian family is undoubtedly one of crisis, but by passionately pursuing God's principles there is an immense amount of hope. Over time, His principles on love, discipline, and training can shape self-centered infants into others-focused men and women of God. As parents, our high calling is to faithfully apply those principles.

Ecclesiastes 12:13-14 Now all has been heard; here is the conclusion of the matter: Fear God and keep His commandments, for this is the whole [duty] of man. For God will bring every deed into judgment, including every hidden thing, whether it is good or evil.

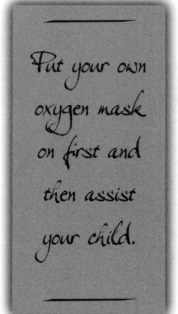

Put your own oxygen mask on first and then assist your child.

Consider the above verse. Before takeoff in an airplane, they always tell you that, in the event of an emergency, you should put your own oxygen mask on first and then assist your child. This is also good advice spiritually. Make sure that you are actively seeking God first and then assist your children. After all, parenting is about the parent.

Parenting is not always black and white. Some people may be looking for more specific input and want to know exactly what to do in every circumstance, for each age, and for each unique child. Not only is that impossible to write, but it misses the point. God has given me wisdom for my kids. *You* need to get wisdom from God for *your* kids. Information can come from other sources, but wisdom comes from God.

To find discussion questions and other articles and resources from Steve and Kathleen Nelson, visit www.premeditatedparenting.net. If you have specific questions you would like us to address, you can send them to us through the 'contact us' page on that website.

Another website with many great articles is Rick Whitney's www.gcnwdads.com. Rick's book *Growing up Whitney* offers a great deal of good, sound parenting advice, especially for older kids.

While you can find thousands of other books on parenting, I'd like to remind you again that gaining more knowledge is not the key to successful parenting. Make sure you are putting more energy into implementing sound parenting principles in your home than you are in finding more information.

I want to thank you for reading through to the end. I hope that you were encouraged and spurred on to pursue God more wholeheartedly. I pray that we will be partners in raising the next generation of believers who will run hard after God. God bless you deeply.

Hebrews 6:10 God is not unjust; He will not forget your work and the love you have shown Him as you have helped His people and continue to help them.